"For decades Phil Callaway has mad[...] This new book is a welcome event."

Max Lucado
pastor and bestselling author

"Callaway could write about owning a shrew and I'd be entertained, amused, and taught something profound. I had no idea we could learn so much from dogs and have this much fun doing so. This book is tender, uplifting, and funny."

Dr. Kevin Leman
author of *Have a Happy Family by Friday*

"Phil Callaway has the extraordinary gift of writing about ordinary life in a way that makes you laugh, cry, reflect, and gain hope—all in the same paragraph. This book might inspire you to get a dog. It will definitely compel you to live a better life."

Richard Blackaby
author of *Experiencing God at Home*
and *Customized Parenting in a Trending World*

"If laughter is the best medicine, Phil is the best apothecary. In this wonderful book about the goodness of a dog, he serves up humor in huge doses and somehow manages to be profound and hilarious in a single breath. Read this story of the two Mojos and prepare to get your own mojo back."

Mark Buchanan
author of *Your Church Is Too Safe*

"*Tricks My Dog Taught Me* made me laugh over and over. And in the vulnerability of that laughter, Phil managed to tug at my heart and challenge my soul. This book will stay with you a long time—it's a refreshing and truthful companion on a life-journey that can be scary and exhausting."

Rick Lawrence
executive editor of *Group Magazine*
author of *Sifted* and *Shrewd*

"Dogs teach us about life, death, and everything in between. Phil Callaway supplies the laughter. Don't miss this long walk with a good friend."

Chris Fabry
author and radio host

"Phil Callaway has done it again. In his oddball yet endearing and deeply resonant way, he connects with our human experience and gives light, laughter, insight, and spiritual encouragement. Even if you're not a dog person, you'll love this book."

Ellen Vaughn
author of *Choosing to See* and *It's All About Him*

"I don't have a dog, but reading *Tricks My Dog Taught Me* awakened me to the homespun wisdom other peoples' dogs can teach me. I guffawed so loudly, my airplane seatmates wanted in on the joke."

Connie Cavanaugh
author of *Following God One Yes at a Time*

"Thank God for another wonderful work by Phil Callaway! Along with lots of laugh-out-loud humor, Phil delivers sage advice that will inspire, inform, and enlighten you."

Charles Marshall
author of *The Seven Powers of Success*

"What a fun read! I loved this book and smiled all the way through. This is pleasant, relaxing, insightful. Easy to read, yet full of truth!"

Carl Madearis
author of *Speaking of Jesus*

tricks
my
dog
taught me

PHIL CALLAWAY

HARVEST HOUSE PUBLISHERS
EUGENE, OREGON

Cover photos © Annette Sheff, Martin Allinger, Lobke Peers, Daniiel / Shutterstock

Cover by Left Coast Design, Portland, Oregon

This book contains stories in which people's names and some details of their situations have been changed to protect their privacy.

> For David,
> my wise and discerning nephew
> who has read each of my books multiple times.
> Lover of life and God.
> But not a big fan of dogs.
> Yet.

TRICKS MY DOG TAUGHT ME

Copyright © 2015 Phil Callaway
Published by Harvest House Publishers
Eugene, Oregon 97402
www.harvesthousepublishers.com

Library of Congress Cataloging-in-Publication Data
    Callaway, Phil, 1961-
    Tricks my dog taught me / Phil Callaway.
      pages cm
    ISBN 978-0-7369-5946-9 (pbk.)
    ISBN 978-0-7369-5947-6 (eBook)
    1. Virtues—Anecdotes. 2. Social skills—Anecdotes. 3. Human-animal relationships—Anecdotes. 4. Dogs—Anecdotes. 5. Christian life—Anecdotes. 6. Callaway, Phil, 1961—Anecdotes. I. Title.
    BJ1521.C1689 2015
    242—dc23

2014024310

Printed in the United States of America

15 16 17 18 19 20 21 22 23 / VP-JH / 10 9 8 7 6 5 4 3 2 1

Contents

Author's Note

While writing this book, I was accosted by several who snickered at my title and the thought of a dog teaching us anything worthwhile. "You haven't met my dog," was how they put it. One confessed, "My dog barks at everything but did nothing when a burglar showed up. I think he helped him carry stuff out. What can I learn from that? Kindness? Servanthood?" Another divulged that his dog routinely lies in front of the tires of his parked car and turns up his nose at dog food, preferring the neighbor's kitty litter box. "We would never allow that behavior in our children," he said.

And he was right. Some of the characteristics we observe in our dogs should not be emulated. For one thing, dogs are incorrigible liars. "Let me outside!" they beg with a grin. "I won't touch the garbage!" But they do touch the garbage. "Take me with you!" they say with their tails. "I won't be a problem!" But they will be a problem.

Dogs are perjurers.

They are also among the world's most adept con artists. They can pick your wallet clean, determine when you sleep and when you rise, bite a million Americans a year, and determine which friends are welcomed and which are snarled at.[1]

Dogs are freeloaders.

They steal unattended cookies, mark your territory as theirs, and bark at hair dryers, violins, ornamental cats, and anything that moves faster than a toddler.

Certain dogs have been known to commandeer and hold hostage entire households. An acquaintance, whose name I shall wisely conceal, walks on eggshells in his own home. He tiptoes around his snarling schnauzer, fearful of disturbing its sleep. The dog adores the man's wife but will sometimes try to keep him from her, guarding doorways and barking wildly when he enters a room. His theme song is "Who Let the Dogs In?" The schnauzer has this man exactly where he wants him. He's playing him like the bagpipes.

The ancient Romans used the word *Canis* to mean "parasite, hanger-on." But most naysayers will admit that, if nothing else, dogs are brilliant at discovering a chink in our armor, of weaseling their way into our hearts. Who wouldn't admire the cunning of a creature with so many woeful habits that is allowed to share the front seat of our cars?

This is the story of one of those dogs. And how that dog changed a family. Forever.

1

Sometimes Love Means
We're Not All There

For many months a picture clung to our fridge. It was a school assignment brought home by our son Jeffery. He'd finished it on time. He'd received stellar marks. I was proud. And a little surprised. At the top he had written, "Wut I wont for Krismus." Below the words was a tree etched in crayon and crowned with a yellow star. Beneath the tree was a gopher. Or a sweater perhaps. I wasn't sure.

"All I wont is a dag," it said.

His teacher, Miss Plett, corrected the spelling and gave the boy an A minus.

Thanks to my wife, the artwork stayed there, causing a small lump to form in my throat with each glass of juice, each midnight snack.

"But, honey," I protested, "with all that's going on in our lives, there's no way." My wife didn't say much. She just kept it on exhibit from November to July with Miss Plett's comment at the top—"I hope this works, Jeffery."

It took about four years, but finally it did.

On a rainy August evening, Jeffery, his sister, Rachael, and his brother, Stephen, couldn't stop grinning as we stood before an indoor kennel.

Selecting the family pet is no cakewalk. You stand before a litter of three squint-eyed little troublemakers, and with one simple nod of your head, you must neglect two of them.

I examined the scoundrels. Number One was a robust little rogue with ink-black eyes, puffed-out chest, and ample attitude. He was a manly dog with real possibilities. With any luck, I could make something of him.

Number Two nudged him aside, almost smiled at me, and then bit his younger sister. I'm no dog's fool. The smile was as fake as a Hong Kong Rolex. "Not him," said Stephen past his braces. Teenagers can spot a poser a mile away.

The owner told us the female was already taken, so we were left with Mr. Attitude, the boy cub with "pick me" eyes.

"This is it?" I asked, which didn't come out right. I knew what it was. It was a setup. My wife, Ramona, had brought me here with our three children—thirteen, eleven, and ten—all of them prepped and prepared to vote. To think the decision was up to me was a brief fantasy I allowed myself.

"Well," said the owner, "there's this little…" and she reached into the pocket of her hoodie. An ear flopped out and then retreated. "Come on," she coaxed. "He doesn't like the light." Her voice was apologetic, the voice you use when your sister won't emerge from her room for a blind date you've been party to all week.

"We've named him Elvis. He's the runt. Whines a lot. Teeth are crooked. Can't get much for him. Think we'll just keep him."

"May I?" I can't remember which child said it, but all three stepped forward together and reached out as if they'd rehearsed.

Elvis dug his claws into the hoodie, but the owner finally tugged from her pocket a whimpering, diminutive fur-ball—part Ewok, part kitten. Toffee brown at the shoulders, his milk-chocolate kneesocks rose above boots of white.

I cringed. Like Elvis, I'd been dragged along on this venture. I didn't mind dogs, but I had no time for one. Besides, I'd always had large dogs, manly dogs, dogs your friends would address as Bud before bending respectfully to scratch their ears. It helped a little that this was a boy dog. But he had no spirit. Disgruntled at being unpocketed, he promptly warmed up his feeble vocal chords and emitted the soft, mournful howl of an animal deprived of mother's milk. Then he piddled on my son's arm.

"Hmm…" I smiled. "My wife doesn't want a boy. They're not so easy, you know?"

Ramona snickered. "You're not kidding," she muttered. We were wedged in the middle of a substantial argument that day, and I thought the snicker had a bit of an edge to it.

The kids quickly warmed to the little wimp though. "Let's…" It was all my daughter could manage as she cradled him. Looking at me, she batted her eyes. "Can we? Please?" I was fine until then. When she batted her eyes I was cheese in a barbecue.

And so it was that we found ourselves driving home with a hound the size of my hand howling in the backseat. As the frightened howl took on increasingly robust proportions, I muttered, "Who's gonna feed him?"

"We will!" came the children's chorus.

"Who's gonna walk him?"

"We will!"

"Who's gonna clean the messes?"

Dead silence except for the whimpering.

"I can't hear you. Who's gonna clean the messes?"

"Mom is!" said Jeffery.

Ramona smiled.

"So," I said through my teeth in a voice only audible in the front seat, "we just spent hundreds of dollars. Dog. Kennel. Food. Shots."

"But look at the kids' faces," my wife said. "Plus he was on sale. Remember?"

"A discounted dog," I said, pulling into our driveway and shaking my head. "A Malteze-shih tzu."

We had a rule in those days. No one gets out of the van until we complete a silly family tradition, fast fading as the kids grew older.

"Do you know why we're here?" I asked.

They responded together, all of them looking at the dog. "Because we're not all there."

I couldn't have summed it up better myself. Were we crazy? This dog could not have arrived at a more inopportune time.

2

Home Is Where My People Are—and Food

I wondered what the dog thought of his new cappuccino-colored house on Eighth Street, its yard littered with bicycles and skateboards. I wouldn't have to wait long. His first act was to toddle off to the backyard, glance sneakily back at me, and wiggle under our garden shed. Bent low, I craned my neck to see what he was up to. Scooting the length of the shed, he pulled his back paws through an escape hatch at the other end. How a six-inch mutt could move so fast, I had no idea. From there, some sixth sense steered him due west toward the bungalow where his mother lived a mile away. The kids laughed as I tracked him down. "Go, Dad!" they yelled.

Finally I corralled and held up the tiny creature. "Stay," I commanded, as you would a toddler. The pup squirmed and looked past me. "I don't want to put you in the kennel," I threatened, nodding at the blue cage-like box on our back deck. The dog squirmed some more, so I let him down. He rolled over, hoping for a scratch. Three sets of hands obliged.

From day one, my expectations for the dog were low. Be clean, loveable, pettable, and loyal. Find me charming. Know that I am the alpha male. The leader of the pack. I am to be obeyed and, if necessary, feared. Under no circumstance are you to chew table legs, slippers, or dress shoes. Guests are not for sniffing, licking, or lunging upon. The trash can is not a buffet. The carpet is not for dragging bones across. Nor bottoms. The neighbor's kitty litter box is not a cookie jar.

For all my gruffness, the animal seemed to know I have been a dog person all my life. A pushover. A softy. With the exception of a few years here and there, we always seemed to have a spare dog around the house. Most were big dogs. Dogs a kid could ride. And feed hay. Mom seemed to think that a house wasn't a home until you threw in a set of four legs and a waggly tail.

The first was Inky, a jet-black terrier with mournful eyes and a lopped tail. Inky was in trouble from the start. I brought him along for hide-and-seek only once. He was kicked out. "Unfair advantage," said Steve Porr. "Leave the dog at home." Inky's major downfall was his fondness for surprising people. Folks strolling by our house late at night, gazing upward, admiring the northern lights, thanking God for his awesome creation, had no idea how fast they could run until Inky showed them. That was his gift, I suppose. Bringing out the best in people. Helping them scream their loudest, run their fastest, and write the most articulate letters to my parents.

When I asked my busy father what happened to Inky, he said, "Sold him to a glue factory." Mom was more wordy about it. She said they found a better home for him on a farm, where he could run free. It helped me sleep at night, thinking of Inky reclining on the floor of the glue factory after a stroll in the grass and a drink from a stream.

After a brief hiatus, we visited the farm of Mr. Yule, a kindhearted Tennessean, renowned for his ornate carvings and substantive collection of dogs. Inky wasn't there, but everywhere there were red dogs, panting, and pouncing. With some prodding from Mom and negotiations with Mr. Yule, Dad handed over what seemed to me a fortune. Before I knew it I was in the backseat of our station wagon with an Irish setter named Lady. She was regal on the surface but drooled like a leaky tap. I came to love that dog, but it was the most disobedient animal God ever created. By Thursday I thought Dad might go back to Mr. Yule, buy a gun, and shoot the dog. He didn't. But many a night I walked our street in my pajamas calling her name loudly—"Lady! Lady!" I was a kid at the time. This is not something you want to be caught doing when you're a little older.

We were a churchgoing family, and one Sunday we arrived home to discover Lady had eaten the soles off our shoes. The preacher had talked of patience that morning, how tribulation helped it work. I don't think Dad was listening. He gave Lady away to Roberta Boutwell, a gorgeous hippy living across the street. Within a week Lady gave birth in the back of Roberta's old station wagon. "They just kept a comin'," she told us. Did they ever. Lady became the tired mother of twelve puppies. I spent that summer asking for one of them. And I spent it barefoot. Shoes were in short supply that year at the Callaway house.

We were dogless for a few summers until I came home to the most glorious surprise of my life—Mojo, a smiling Heinz 57 who would live fifteen fantastic years. It's hard to believe I married during her lifetime because she was just about all the companion a boy could handle. Shy and humble, Mojo was a friend of strangers. Most people in our town knew her. I shut my eyes and I can see her loping toward me—glossy back, white chest, black mask, and brindle on the nape.

When our kids were small I immortalized her, recounting imaginary fables of Mojo at night. Mojo the Superdog. Rescuer of distressed children and the elderly. Able to soar from buildings and land unperturbed while carrying a bundled child in her jaws.

So there in the backyard, with the kids massaging our little Ewok's belly and doling out treats, I asked, "What shall we name him?"

My wife said, "How about Puddles?"

I said, "How about Maher-shalal-hash-baz? That's Hebrew for 'Hurry to the spoils. Hasten to the plunder.'" The kids looked at me like I was wearing a fish on my head.

"A friend of mine has two dogs," I continued. "He named them Sam and Ella." Silence. Jokes you have to explain aren't worth telling.

"What about Dolly?" asked Rachael.

"What about Mojo?" asked one of the boys. The kids all smiled. Mojo seemed to be smiling too. And that was that.

3

When You Don't Get What You Want
Roll with It

Your first night with a puppy is rarely a restful one. In fact, the best place for a new dog to spend his first night is in someone else's laundry room eleven miles from your house. Dog books describe both Maltese and shih tzu puppies as "difficult to housebreak." A friend with a shih tzu told me, "It tends to wheeze a lot. Snores. Has respiratory problems." *Great*, I thought. *It's like Uncle Lenny is moving in for good.*

Sure enough. That first night at our house there was whimpering and bickering. And the dog wasn't easy to deal with either. My wife said, "Stop with the whining." So I did. But not before I reminded her that I had my share of things to whine about.

In the past year we had built a house, acquired a hefty mortgage, and invited my aging parents to live in a spacious one-bedroom suite we built in it. It was Ramona's idea. As Mom and Dad became increasingly unable to care for themselves, she believed that we should do unto our parents as we would have our kids do unto us. So the four of us sat at an ice-cream shop one day, and we told them what we were thinking. Smiles came first. Then tears.

Friends asked if we were sure we should do this. Of course we weren't. We just felt it was the right thing to do. What they really meant was, "Are you out of your cotton-pickin' minds?" Yes we were. Our kids were entering the teen years, and it hit me as I finally climbed into bed that with the acquisition of this latest little hitchhiker, these friends had a point.

"Let's run away from home," I suggested. Ramona smiled.

Mojo finally offered us a few seconds of silence, and I wondered what he was into. "I can't believe we did this," I groaned.

"What? The dog?"

"Yes. You know this dog is related to the hound next door?"

"Chewie?"

Chewie was without a doubt the scruffiest, most ill-behaved dog I had ever met. A year older than Mojo, he was bat-eared, ill-tempered, and mean. I had yet to get within six feet of him without the dog going crazy. I mean psychopathic, Cujo crazy.

"Chewie would attack *himself* if no one else was available," I said.

Ramona laughed at the thought of this. In the next room, Mojo was stirring again, letting out a long, mournful howl.

"Dad won't like the dog either."

"Sure he will. Why do you say that?"

"You know. He never cared for dogs. Mom was always the one begging him for us."

"What's not to like?"

"The mess. The barking. The dirty paws."

"I guess we'll see what he thinks in the morning."

Mojo was emitting soft, insincere yipping sounds.

"Did I ever tell you that Mom used to put an alarm clock and hot water bottle under a blanket to help our puppies adapt to their first night in our house? The theory was that the warmth would remind them of their mothers."

"What was the alarm clock for?"

"I can't remember. She got the idea from a dog book I think. Maybe the ticking was why our dogs were so paranoid."

"Do you think the bathroom idea will work?" It was my turn to laugh. We had followed a friend's counsel to put the pup on a soft blanket in our master bathroom, shield the floor with newspaper, and call the friend for more advice in a day or two. I had stuffed a housecoat against the door to muffle the sounds. It seemed to amplify them. The latest addition to our family was softly scratching our bathroom door now, slowly, one paw at a time.

I glanced at my watch. Two in the morning. The earplugs turned loud scratching to soft scratching, so we lay there, recounting our day.

"This is kind of nice," said Ramona. "We haven't…talked much lately."

I pretended to be asleep. She knew better.

"How are you doing?"

It seemed like the time to tell her. "The doctor wants me on the meds," I said.

A few years earlier I had experienced a crippling burnout that slowly spiraled into despair. I seldom slept now, anxious, agitated, negative, and numb. I knew that depression was something my family had battled through the years, the kind that paralyzes and debilitates, testing the limits of your relationships, your job, your faith. As a kid I had a recurring dream in which I was walking down the street and the sidewalk slowly turned to quicksand, sucking me downward. The dream had come to life the last year.

As a humorist my job was to bring joy to the lives of others. The hypocrisy was not lost on me. But for brief interludes, the joy was gone.

I would do my best to go along with it, but adding a dog to the mix could only make things worse. Dog hair on the couch was the least of my worries.

My wife eventually had enough of the scratching and whining in the bathroom. She opened the door, flipped on the light, and picked up the dog. I saw her frown and lift the pup higher.

"He's a girl," she said. And he was.

4

Humans Will Dress You Up
Just Love Them

Mojo, I want you to meet your grandfather." Neither the squirming pup nor my aging dad seemed all that impressed with my introduction the next morning. Dad bent down, scratched the dog's chin, and asked if he could borrow some cereal. It was a start. Though I hoped the dog would grow on both of us, there was a bit of my dad in me too.

Our friends Jane and Al were coming for dinner that night. Whereas Dad tolerated dogs, they couldn't stand them. Small ones anyway. I wondered why.

When they arrived I was smothering four medium rares in sauce on the backyard barbecue. Jane brought a fruit salad, and Al was swatting mosquitoes. Mojo introduced them to all six inches of herself by running mad circles around them and then sitting down and staring longingly up at the barbecue. "They can be fun, I suppose," said Al. "But…she reminds me of Precious."

The kids were out with friends, and it was nice to enjoy some adult conversation. "Who's Precious?" I asked as I brought the steaks to the table.

"Precious is my parents' dog," said Jane, and the strange story unfolded from there. Since this little bundle of Chihuahua arrived, Jane and the grandchildren had barely seen Grandpa and Grandma. They had missed their grandchildren's graduations and birthdays and even Christmas. "Last year they didn't make it to our daughter's wedding."

"Unbelievable," I said.

"Yep," Al leaned forward and laughed. "They gave the grandkids away because the dog was allergic to them."

Jane wasn't laughing. Though she and Al flew to visit when they could, she missed her parents.

"Precious doesn't travel so well," she continued. "His plumbing malfunctions at the very mention of air or car travel. No one is good enough to dog-sit. So the three of them stay home together. Home is where Precious is."

"They plan this dog's meals in advance. On a chart." More shaking of Al's head. "They buy Halloween outfits and liver biscotti and oatmeal shampoo for sensitive skin. Precious wears a necklace with bone charms hanging from it." Al hiked his eyebrows at the memory of this.

"They weren't this way with Max, their previous dog," added Jane, with just a touch of defensiveness. "But when Max died, they joined a pet-loss bereavement group. It was moderated by a full-time veterinary social worker who talked about the five stages of loss and grief. And it wasn't just grief. They felt guilt too. The vet told them they could have saved Max's life with a kidney transplant. It would have cost something like $8000—if they could find a donor."

"They missed your daughter's wedding?" my wife asked.

Somehow Mojo had found a way onto Jane's lap and was being scratched behind her ears. "They said they couldn't leave Precious alone. Said she suffers from separation anxiety."

"You can set up a small camera now and watch your dog from work," I suggested, partly kidding. "They could eavesdrop to make sure he's okay."

Al was shaking his head again. "Don't tell them. They'll do it. This dog is a fur baby."

The sun was slowly dipping behind the Rockies. "Is this why you haven't been a big fan of dogs?" I asked.

"I guess," said Al.

"But we can't blame the dogs."

"I agree," said Al. "But did you know you can pay for dog walkers, dog groomers, and dog-friendly hotels? Their dog is on puppy Prozac.

They feed it organic dog food. Filtered water. There's just so much overindulgence."

I couldn't argue. "Americans spend more than $60 billion a year on their pets." Al had clearly been studying these things. "You can get acupuncture sessions for $150 an hour. I just read about a Greenwich Village couple that spent $3500 for hydrotherapy treatments for a twelve-year-old shih tzu."

Mojo cocked her head as if she knew we were talking about her kind.

"We're getting her fixed," said Ramona. "How much is that?"

I hadn't a clue.

Mojo looked at my wife as if she were saying, "Don't fix me, just love me."

"Dogs are like honorary children now." Al was on a roll. "Used to be you called your dog Lucky or Spot or Scamp. Now people call them kids' names. Jake. Chloe. Bella. You didn't name your dog Danny when I was a kid. People would have thought you were crazy. They have pet cemeteries. That's where Grandpa and Grandma buried Max. They sent us a picture of the tombstone. It says something like, 'Max, our baby. Run free with friends and God.'"

Cheesecake was a welcome interruption. Mojo was leaning hard into Jane's scratches. Suddenly Al laughed. "So last November Jane's parents asked us what we wanted for Christmas," he said. "We hardly ever see them, so we asked for a picture of the two of them that we could frame and put above our mantel."

It was Jane's turn to shake her head.

"Christmas morning our kids opened a package about three feet by four feet." Al stretched his arms out to show us. "It was the picture we asked for. Nice frame. They even had it taken by a professional photographer. But they were holding the dog, and get this—" The two finished the sentence together. "They're both *looking* at the dog!"

Al laughed, but Jane wasn't seeing the humor quite yet. Precious had become this couple's entire social support network. Who needs grandchildren and church and Facebook when you have a Chihuahua?

I thought of my childhood dog Mojo. Few friends were better companions. But a dog is far too humble a creature to be worshipped.

"Come on, Jane," Al said. "It's funny. We've gotta laugh."

As we bid them goodnight, I was nursing a stomachache and had no one else to blame for eating a third slice of cheesecake. "If ever you see me dressing this pup in a doggy tuxedo," I said, "promise you'll shoot me."

Jane was still holding the pup, cuddling it. "Mind if I take her home?" she said.

And for the first time that night, she laughed.

5

You Need Love, Food, and the D-Word Too

Maybe I'm allergic to the dog," I said to no one as I knelt before an ice-cream bucket, cradling it, groaning, sick as ever I'd been. It was the middle of the night, and as I lifted my blurry eyes from the bucket, my wife's slippers came into view. I do not suffer infirmity well, so she must have been awakened by my groaning. "Sorry, honey. You'll be okay." And the slippers disappeared. I couldn't blame her. Fatigue from running our little asylum was understandable. But some sympathy would have been nice.

The majority of the next hour I spent alone in the bathroom, acquainting myself with that bucket, wishing the cheesecake was back in the pan, thankful we had coated the floor in newspaper. I shouldn't say alone, however. During that woeful hour, only one living creature paid me any notice. A furry little six-inch dog stayed by my side. And when at last I crawled out to the sofa and laid my head to rest, I heard a noise, turned, and saw two tiny paws reaching up at me, clawing the sofa.

"Mojo," I groaned.

The scratching was joined by a soft whimper, so I managed to scoop her up with one hand and plunk her down by my knees. She let out a soft yip and slowly slithered upward onto my chest.

"I am so sick," I moaned. "I think I'm gonna die. You don't wanna be anywhere near me." But she did. She lay there listening to the magnitude of my complaints, the gravity of my circumstances. Her breath came in short bursts, but she stayed put.

And when I awoke to watch the earliest rays of sun paint our wall in crimson with gold tassels, she was still lying there, looking at me as if to say, "You big baby. Stop complaining. You'll be fine."

But I wasn't fine. The entire day I barely moved from the couch. Nor did she. I ate a solitary piece of toast with butter. Mojo helped me. I fell asleep. So did the dog.

I almost wished she would piddle or tear apart a pillow so I could have an excuse not to like her, but she lay there, as close to my chest as she could get. I didn't push her away as I thought I would. Every hour Ramona took her outside and then put her back at my feet. She slithered higher.

Dad knocked on the door just after lunch to visit me in my misery. "How you doing?"

"Horrible," I replied.

He was intrigued by the new dog. "Hello," he said, patting her head. That was the extent of it. He stayed long enough to tell me how much they enjoyed living in our suite and what an answer to prayer it had been. There were tears in his eyes.

"Get some rest," he said as he softly closed the door.

Moments later, Mom dropped by. "So cute," she said.

"Thanks."

She smiled. "You too. But the dog. He's adorable."

"She," I corrected. "He's a she."

"Oh." She scratched the pup's chin and began talking to her in baby talk. I couldn't believe it. My own mother. Registering more concern for the dog than for the fact that I was very likely going to die within hours. Surely the kids would show sympathy.

"Come," I groaned, when they arrived home from school. "I am about to die. It is time to divide the spoils."

Completely ignoring me, they grabbed a few cookies; cooed, cuddled, and cradled the pup; and then scooped her up and left to show their friends.

At dinnertime I summoned the energy to reach for the remote and watch some baseball. Toronto's Blue Jays were losing to someone, and Ramona brought a fresh muffin in hopes it would soothe my stomach. I ate most of it and lay the muffin wrapper beside me. A few pitches later, I looked down to discover that the muffin wrapper had vanished. "Hey," I said. Mojo had crumbs around her mouth. She was guilty as a four-year-old caught in a lie.

"No," I commanded, aware that her cheeks were swollen chipmunk-like. Reaching toward her, I attempted to open her tiny mouth and spare her irritable wrapper syndrome. She snarled and snapped at my hand. The kind, playful animal had become a monster.

"No," I repeated, reaching toward her again. More snarling and snapping.

I calmly repeated my command.

"You will never be in charge," I said, lightly tapping her nose. To paraphrase my mother, "I brought you into this house. I can take you out of it." A dog needs affection, food, and exercise. And an under-rated virtue called discipline too. Mojo closed her eyes and allowed me to fish around and pull from her mouth and throat a sizeable wad of pasty muffin wrapping covered in goop.

She would never snap at me again. Nor would I ever tap her wet little nose.

As darkness descended I no longer felt like death was about to visit. I carried the dog with me to the bedroom, thinking to myself, *She's learned a few things, but I have too. I have spent the day in the company of the world's best psychiatrist. One who sits by my couch and says, "I think you're wonderful." So, like my dog, I need to stop whining, listen up, and just be there.*

"You can't put her there," said Ramona, pointing to the bed and then nodding toward the bathroom. "I put the papers down."

"Sleep tight," I said as I pushed my furry little friend through the bathroom door. She spun around and looked up at me hopefully. "No," I said, waggling my finger. "Be quiet. Go to sleep."

And promptly at a quarter to two, she did.

6

There's a Time to Growl

Shortly after breakfast I called my dog expert friend to tell him that his put-the-pup-in-the-bathroom idea wasn't working. "The dog is sleeping a little more than she did a week ago, but in the morning there are still messes on the newspaper."

"Perfect," he said. "Tonight take away one section of newspaper. And buy thicker earplugs."

It was tough to imagine a creature of such tiny proportions producing the sheer volume of mess this one was capable of producing. A thirty-pound pit bull, perhaps, but not a fur-ball of this size.

Newspaper was strewn about the floor. A barricade had been erected between the kitchen and living room. Stepping over it, I awoke two squeaky toys and kicked over the water dish. A math textbook was missing a corner, and a trail of mucky paw prints led from the pantry to a little bed the kids had made. From a pillow I used to prop myself up and watch TV.

When I mentioned this to an already exasperated Ramona, she unwittingly issued me my first of many lessons the dog was teaching her: "Life gets messy. Let's do the best we can, okay?"

Dad knocked on the door that Saturday and asked how I was. Though I thought he was beginning to like the pup, he seemed to ignore her this time. But dogs are for children anyway, and anyone who says money can't buy happiness has likely forgotten about puppies in August. The kids ran and rolled with her in the yard, and by late morning the following Saturday, they claimed she had learned a trick. If they pushed on her backside while holding up a piece of dried apricot, she sat ever so briefly—as long as they kept pushing on her backside. And if they held the dried fruit above her and drew circles with it, she danced. Within a week they would teach her to sit for real, to lie down, and to shake with the wrong paw.

In hindsight, I was entirely unprepared to have a dog teach us a few tricks too. But it began to happen slowly, first with my children and then with me.

You can learn a hundred things from a dog, some of them good. You don't go to a dog for advice on hygiene or what to eat or how to greet your friends, but by the time September arrived and the earplugs had been discarded and we were down to one small section of newspaper in the bathroom, Mojo discovered something beneath our garden shed and taught my son a trick he will never forget.

In those days Stephen was small for his age and, well, sleek. Skinny you might say. He couldn't play hula hoops with a Cheerio or anything, but the boy was like me at that age—uncommonly thin. With thinness comes merciless teasing, and the school bully had begun to make his life miserable with verbal rants and sometimes fists. Summertime was easier, but the night before school revved up, I saw Stephen's shoulders hunching and traces of tears in his eyes. A few questions from me, and he spilled the whole story. When I learned the bully had crammed my son into a locker on the last day of school, I wanted to find the boy's dad and do some cramming of my own.

"You don't know what it's like to be kicked and pushed," Stephen said.

"I do," I told him. "It's one of the hardest things in life. I'm glad you told me. Thanks. Do you want to know what I've learned?"

"Sure."

"Well, I developed my sense of humor to keep from being beaten up." This didn't seem to help the boy at all.

"I was pushed into a locker once. Stayed in there. Made little growling noises." He brightened at this. "Grandma told me to never hate a bully. She's right. But I'd like you to tell me if it continues. Bullies are just cowards all dressed up. They want you to be as miserable as they are. You're nice, Son. But you're not weak. Now, give me your fist. That's one tough fist. I wouldn't want to meet up with it. I don't ever want you starting a fight. But you can finish one. You're far tougher than you think."

He seemed confused for about two seconds, and then the corners of his mouth turned upward. "Maybe we should have bought a rottweiler," I said.

At this, he laughed.

About that time, Mojo took an unhealthy interest in a gopher living in a hole beneath our garden shed. Each time there was a piercing screech, Mojo made a beeline for the door, wanting outside. And once she caught the scent, she was interested in little else. When the gopher reared its head, she chased him back down the hole. There was one small problem. Literally. Pound for pound, the dog was tinier, and one day while we were having dinner on our back deck, the truth seemed to dawn upon the gopher. He crawled out defiantly and stood straight up, like Goliath mocking David. With dizzying speed, the little dog charged. It happened too fast for us to intervene. She lunged, grabbed the back of the critter's neck, and shook it hard. The gopher went limp. The kids went crazy. "Don't encourage her," I said. But they couldn't stop celebrating David's victory.

The very next Friday Stephen came home lit up like a Christmas tree. The bully had cornered him in the hallway and stepped on one of his shoes so he couldn't move. Finally, Stephen reared back, curled his fist into a tight ball, and let him have it. Socked him in the chin. A few kids cheered. More registered shock. But the bully never touched him again.

He couldn't know that bullying doesn't always end when you get older. But those who have been bullied are better able to recognize it later on, and when they find injustice, they know that neutrality only aids the oppressor. Those courageous enough to stand up, to get help, can change what isn't right. I told him what to do. But a little dog showed him. Maybe Erma Bombeck was right—"Every puppy should have a boy."

I once asked Stephen what would happen if he grew up to be a doctor and he was the only doctor who could save that bully's life. "I'd save his life," he said. And he meant it. Then he smiled. "I'd start by fixing his chin."

That night I summoned the courage to remove the last piece of newspaper from our bathroom.

You Can Stay Where You Are
Or Go Somewhere Else

I awoke one morning to the realization that a small carnivore was attacking my face. My wife had put the pup up to it, and like a calf at a salt lick, Mojo was giving me a thorough going-over.

I was surprised by my response.

I actually smiled.

Which only encouraged them both.

Dogs are incorrigibly happy creatures. Certain breeds may not look the part, but deep down, even a pug has a happy soul. This was the first of many secrets this dog would teach me: From the first moment your eyes open, attack the day with expectancy.

In our survey of more than 300 dog owners, we asked, "How does your dog react when he sees you first thing in the morning?"[1] Sixty-one percent answered, "Goes crazy." Thirty percent said, "Wants something from me." Only 9 percent admitted, "Doesn't seem to notice me." Of those who said their dog didn't seem to notice, many admitted that they largely ignored their animal too.

On any given morning my dog put her entire body into the first act of her day—the greeting. First the shake. Then the snort. Then a leap in the air reaching up to four feet. (Keep in mind, this dog was perhaps eight inches long by now.) Next she rolled over, and when I scratched her sides, she stretched out completely, pawing the carpet, propelling herself in circles, spinning like an upended Jeep. One more snort and she was out the door to do her rain dance. Three times in a circle. Brief squat. Then she charged back to settle in by the kitchen table, where she employed every possible facial feature to guilt me for eating breakfast.

Each and every morning this dog had me at hello.

Many of our surveyed dog owners cheerfully described these early morning encounters almost intimately: "Jumps onto my bed and dives under the covers!" "Wants a hug and a snuggle." "Wags her tail and does a cute grunting thing." "Greets me with a lick." "Rolls over for a tummy scratch." "Brings a toy." "Yawns, stretches, and kisses my face."

Is there a better way to start your day than with a whole-body greeting? I don't mean some New Age positivity, but unbridled enthusiasm that takes leave of its senses.

At first her expectant positivity annoyed me. Why? Perhaps I thought, *Hey, you don't know the bumps I received yesterday or what I'm dealing with today. You don't know the warts and bruises I've been nursing in my dreams or the hurts I've been hanging on to from childhood.* But while being attacked by a three-pound fur-ball, I knew one thing—right now it didn't matter. Yes, there was much about my day that I may not have liked, but was being morose going to help me in some small way to face it?

Soon that annoyance turned to intrigue, the intrigue to envy, and the envy to imitation.

One morning I found that Mojo had piddled on the corner of an old box crammed with my parents' books. While rescuing the books, I happened upon a biography from the 1950s. It was the story of Fanny Jane Crosby.

Born in Putnam County, New York, Fanny developed inflammation of the eyes at six weeks. With the family doctor away, another man—posing as a certified doctor—prescribed hot mustard poultices. The treatment left her blind, and the doctor disappeared. A few months later, Crosby's father died. Her love of poetry began early, and at eight years of age, she wrote a short poem that would echo her lifelong refusal to feel sorry for herself.

> Oh, what a happy soul I am,
> Although I cannot see!
> I am resolved that in this world
> Contented I will be.
>
> How many blessings I enjoy
> That other people don't,
> To weep and sigh because I'm blind
> I cannot, and I won't!

I once joked about being unable to put down a book I was reading on gravity. But this time it was true. I read the book to my wife in two sittings, marveling at Fanny's tenacity and courage. She wrote more than 1000 poems—some for presidents—and more than 9000 songs. [2] When asked about her blindness, Crosby reportedly said that without her affliction she might not have had so good an education or so great an influence and certainly not so fine a memory. [3]

When I laid down the book, I knew I could never be the same.

I would start the day mindful of new mercies and new possibilities. I would not lick people or jump on them, but like my dog, I would embrace each day with gusto and see where it took me.

I tossed Mojo a bite of peanut butter and honey on twelve-grain oat bread, looked across the table, and said to my wife, "You look fantastic! Thanks for breakfast. I love your dress; is it new?"

She was stunned. "I've had it awhile," she said, blushing. "Thanks." Then her eyes lowered. "Have you checked your newspaper?"

"No. How come?"

"Well, Mojo hasn't been going in the bathroom. She's almost trained. But we trained her to go on newspaper. She's been going on yours."

8

Sniff Out New Possibilities

A pup is an almost unending source of playfulness. Everything is sniffable, lickable, and scratchable. Everything is to be upturned, piddled on, and pounced on. Each new sight is a treasure chest of wonder. Squirrels. Trees. Bugs. A blade of grass. Cracks in the sidewalk.

But one Saturday, the play was gone. I was stumbling about the kitchen, bleary-eyed, having already received bad news on my smartphone. Mojo lay on a mat as I prepared breakfast. Her eyes slowly followed me, but her tail was down, ears flattened. I offered her a lick of peanut butter. She blinked and turned away. Finally, pulling herself up, she stretched and ambled toward her water dish. There she threw up and slowly staggered back to the mat, her hindquarters out of sync with the rest of her. "Who put wine in her dish?" I muttered as I cleaned the mess.

By late morning she still hadn't moved, so I called the vet.

"Has she eaten anything unusual?" asked Kathy.

"I don't think so."

"Ask your wife and kids and call me back."

During the interrogations everyone shook their head except Jeffery. He looked down and whispered, "Uh-oh."

"What did you feed her?"

"Uh...some candy."

"How much?"

"Just a few licorice sticks."

"Black licorice?"

"Yep. And chips. She likes 'em with dip."

"Uh...not a great idea."

"Nuts." I thought he said it out of regret.

"We need to be careful what we give her."

"Nuts," he said again. "She likes those too."

"You fed her nuts?"

"Macadamias."

"How many."

"A handful. Maybe more."

I phoned the vet and told on him.

"Ah," said Kathy. "Macadamias are no good. They make some dogs weak and give them tremors and a fever."

"What should we do?"

"Just wait. She should be fine."

And she was. Sunday morning Mojo's nose awoke before the rest of her and gradually slipped her body into hyperdrive. By breakfast she was discovering things I couldn't with that nose of hers. I smelled coffee and toast. She smelled a world rich with the scent of houseplants and discarded clothing and yesterday's trash beneath the sink—an inviting and delightful cocktail for the nose. In the same way I saw the world, my dog smelled it.

For lunch, Mom and Dad had tuna-melt sandwiches with us on the back deck. Dad seemed unimpressed, but Mom laughed at the dog's enthusiasm. The backyard had become a vast wonderland for this creature. Five aging pines offered shade and sap and ants. There were gophers beneath the shed, bugs hiding in the garden, and birds in the trees just a few feet above her head.

I was reading a book about dogs by then, so I attempted to impress them with what I'd learned. "A dog's nose is one of the great marvels of creation," I said. "Dogs see with their noses the way we see with our eyes." I described to them how dogologists who study airflow to the nose are bug-eyed about their findings. Muscles deep in the nostrils draw air inside, displacing the air already there through slits in the side of the nose, pulling new scents in, helping the sniffer smell. The tissue on the inside is enveloped by receptor sites, each with hairs standing sentinel to catch sniffable molecules. Our noses have about six million of these receptor sites. A sheepdog has more than two hundred million. A beagle's sense of smell may be millions of times more sensitive than ours.

"That's why you can't fool her at night," said my wife.

I am an incurable snacker. Most midnights my insomnia nudges me from beneath the warm sheets to tiptoe to the kitchen past a sleeping dog. There I build myself a plateful of cheese and crackers, topping it with pickles and whatever fruit I can find, and then sneak back into bed. About 90 percent of the time my wife lies undisturbed, softly breathing. Sometimes she awakes and utters something incoherent. But I have yet to fool my dog even once. The nose knows. Her olfactory recess is a labyrinth of paper-thin bones lined with millions of scent receptors, and the cheese receptor may be the largest.

Anyone who thinks a dog can't count should give the dog two treats and leave a third in his pocket. We can't hide the fact that a peanut butter sandwich is on the table. If it's been there four days, to my dog it's only getting all the more inviting.

Dad was mildly impressed to learn a little more about dogs, and I watched him reach down and scratch Mojo's ears.

I was increasingly impressed too. The childlike wonder of a dog began to intrigue me. On any given day I overlooked so much that my dog smelled and heard and saw. Driving to work I was oblivious to sights I once found intriguing—people, trees, billboards, even the sunrise. When I brought my dog along I noticed things long forgotten. I put her in the car, and I may lose my hearing when she barks at anything or nothing at all. But for her, the world is crammed with possibilities.

Walking the dog that afternoon, I said to Ramona, "When did I lose the wonder? When did I stop being interested?" She didn't say much. Perhaps she had known me long enough to wonder that too. I could blame stress and the challenges of life, career, and family, but the choice is always up to me.

There was a time when we applauded pilots for a smooth landing. No longer. The last time I saw a pilot receive such praise was when the oxygen masks fell and we landed in fog so thick we couldn't see the tarmac when we pulled up to the gate.

In watching Mojo, it dawned on me that if I wanted the wonder to return, I must stop overlooking things and taking them for granted. I would seize every opportunity to feel the wind on my face. To turn off my smartphone and take an active interest in the world around me. I would thank God for my five senses and use them.

Sadly, most of my thoughts had become consumed with concern about past failures and regrets, things I'd done poorly, things done to me. I knew that the remedies for my ailments were more complex, but watching a tiny dog's sniffer that day, I also knew where to start. I would not mope about what is past, about what is done. I would find out what's beyond that next hill and sniff out new possibilities. I wouldn't miss what is happening now because I was too busy looking back. I would chase the ball. I would dive in.

9

Don't Quit

Noah Took Six Months to Find a Parking Spot

One afternoon a lifelong friend came into my office and dropped a cartoon on my desk. In it, a prune-faced man was talking to the doctor. The caption read, "What do you mean I've got an ulcer? I don't get ulcers, I give them."

He had penciled my name above the sour patient.

I was not particularly amused, but I pretended to be. "Are you serious? Is that me?"

He laughed. "No. But…well, maybe. Just a little."

"I'm sorry. I'm just tired. Plus my smile doesn't work." Admittedly, he had a point. At times I felt that life was beginning to unravel.

Four years earlier my wife experienced her first grand mal seizure. I know of few events more terrifying for both the patient and those who love her. Despite a thousand prayers and the efforts of a dozen doctors, the seizures continued. Sometimes they left us alone for a week. Or a month. More often they arrived several times a day, knocking the stuffing out of us. Doctors shook their heads and wrote referral notices. Friends recommended remedies, and I appreciated their concern. But I told no one that deep within me, resentment was growing like cancer. How could I hold down a job, care for a wife and aging parents—to say nothing of raising three kids and this new little mutt? Did God even care?

As autumn turned to winter, the walls began to inch in on me. One night as I lay awake, a thought occurred to me. *Run, Callaway. Make a dash for it.*

A man I played softball with had done this. One week he was there, and the next he wasn't. We filled his spot in center field. Life went on. Perhaps this would be the shortest cut to peace. The thought jolted me when it hit. Of course I knew what was right, but sometimes what is wrong causes our stomachs to jump in anticipation.

Jeffery was struggling in school, and I kept offering him hypocritical bits of advice. Just hang in there. It'll get better. Be faithful. Don't quit.

Rick Warren's book *The Purpose-Driven Life* had just been released, and I was privileged to spend an hour with him, recording an interview for print, reviewing a book that would sell thirty million copies.

"I have a friend who's going through some tough stuff," I told Rick. "What would you say to him?"

"I'd say that God never wastes a hurt. Of all the different experiences you have in life, the most important ones are the painful ones. They're not accidents. The very thing that you resent the most, that you wish had never happened, the thing you're most ashamed of, the thing that has hurt you the most, is the very thing God wants to use in your life. It may be the start of your greatest ministry to others."

"You're thinking it's me," I smirked.

"Yep."

"You're right."

"I thought so," laughed Rick. "Listen. I don't know what you're going through, but don't give up. Who can help the parents of a Down syndrome child better than the parents of a Down syndrome child? Who can help an addict better than somebody who's been an addict? Who can help somebody who's been raped or molested more than somebody who's suffered rape and molestation? God uses all these things to shape us for serving him."

I badly needed to hear this.

"Temptation," said Rick, "is always an opportunity to do good, not just bad."

Spring was almost here, and according to my daughter, Mojo had begun to nudge the weigh scale needle past the five-pound mark. One night the kids called me, "Come look." They were kneeling at the top of the stairs, coaxing and cheering for the dog. "Come on, come on!"

Don't ask me why, but Mojo had a toy cat between her teeth and was endeavoring to drag it up the stairs, something she'd tried almost daily for two weeks. It looked impossible. The stuffed cat was at least her weight and twice her size. But the stubborn dog would not quit. She tried pushing it. Tossing it. Dragging the cat sideways. She tried pulling it backward and ended up tumbling head over heels in a heap. When she let it go, she looked up at us and wagged her tail.

"Come on," Rachael said. "You can do it."

But the dog couldn't even get the cat up one stair. And there were fourteen of them. We counted. But like those toy punching clowns that bounce back up each time you sock them, she wouldn't quit.

"Come on, come on," the kids cheered.

And then it happened. She backed up, lifted her head as high as it would go, and made a run for it. One faltering stride at a time she lugged that cat up fourteen stairs. It was a miracle of tenacity and courage and a lesson in perseverance. We shouted and cheered. Jeffery and I rewarded her with muffin chunks and apricots. Maybe because we were the ones who most needed her example.

That night I finished editing the interview with Rick Warren, and words I'd heard before suddenly made sense. "The most damaging aspect of contemporary living is short-term thinking. Don't give up. Resolute perseverance in times of difficulty and distress is proof that we're authentic servants of God. Remember how far you've come, not just how far you have to go."

Talent and genius and opportunity and education are wonderful gifts. But none can take the place of determination. Let what happened happen. Then get up and get going.

I didn't admit it out loud quite yet, but I was beginning to like this dog.

10

Go Ahead and Howl

A dog seems to celebrate each season of the year but none more than the return of summer. Playing fetch. Stretching out in the sun. Lying beneath the barbecue, hoping that something will slip through the cracks. After one of those barbecues, we had a family picture taken. The girls were color coordinated, the smiles were perfect, the laughter was plentiful. But when I posted the photo on a social networking site, the comments were less about the humans than the pup. "The dog is laughing!" was the common consensus. Sure enough, the photographer had caught Mojo mid-yawn. To us humans, she was tilting her head back, laughing. But do dogs laugh?

Max Eastman believed, "Dogs laugh, but they laugh with their tails."

For years behavioral biologists agreed that laughter was an emotional expression unique to humans. Now the consensus is that dogs have what can be called a laugh, a spontaneous breathy eruption spit forth in response to something surprising or funny. This pant has been measured only when dogs play or try to entice us to play with them. Like the laughter of humans, it is a sign of terrific enjoyment, it is contagious, and it reduces stress. In fact, when sound bites of dog laughter are played at animal shelters, they reduce pacing, barking, and other signs of doggy stress.

We love to anthropomorphize, attributing human characteristics to the pets we love as though their emotional lives were entirely reflected in ours. I do not think that dogs sit around telling doggie jokes and laughing until they hyperventilate. But if a dog does not laugh, it undoubtedly has the capacity to make humans laugh, prolonging our lives and perkifying our days.

When asked, "Does your dog make you laugh?" 96 percent of our three hundred dog owners were almost insulted.[1] "Yes!" they replied. Only twelve checked the No box, and none of them explained why. Here were just a few of the ways Mojo made me laugh.

- She fell asleep on her back, legs in the air.

- She spent close to an hour howling at a ceramic rabbit we purchased as a lawn ornament.

- One day for no reason at all, she dragged a tree branch up the front step. It was ten times her size.

- After a bath she propelled herself from carpet to carpet, snorting and plunging her nose into couches and shoes and blankets—anything that would ease her bad hair day and remove the horrible smell of Extra Fortified Vanilla Baby Shampoo.

Almost single-handedly, this little dog began to bring the laughter back to my life. Arriving home, I would climb from the car and walk through the front yard when suddenly a fur-ball would blur past me, racing in frantic circles for no reason at all, madly dashing between my legs, ears pinned back, reversing course, and then doing it again. If you can observe such behavior without laughing, no psychologist can help you.

Dogs teach us that when you get the chance, go ahead and howl. They bring out the goofy in us. Take these actual classified ads as evidence.

Free Yorkshire Terrier
Eight years old. Hateful little dog. Bites.

Free Puppies
Half cocker spaniel, half sneaky neighbor's dog.

Found: Dirty White Dog
Looks like a rat—been out awhile. Better be a reward.

The power of laughter to bring joy and happiness to life is indisputable. Just ask 288 dog owners why their dog makes them laugh. Some listed ten or more ways. Here were the most common.

- "He picks up the dog dish and brings it to me if it's empty."
- "Her tail wags so hard her entire backside swings."
- "She's a pug! What's not to laugh at?"
- "Thinks he's human. Tries to push my son off his chair so he can sit with the family at dinner."
- "If he's in trouble, he hides his head and won't look at you."
- "Talks to me if I'm not paying attention to him."
- "A howl if he wants outside. A high-pitched bark if he's mad. A low bow-wow if he's 'talking.' A fierce bark if someone is outside the window."
- "Thinks the fireplace is an exit."
- "When I sing, he sings with me."
- "Milk jugs are his favorite toy. He chases them around the house and can never get a grip on them."
- "She plays fetch—by herself."
- "Chews on empty water bottles. It sounds like a popcorn popper."
- "Tries to herd our car."
- "She 'happy piddles' when my husband comes home. (He doesn't laugh at this.)"
- "Buries bones and toys in the corners of the room."
- "Gets so excited at the slightest hint of cheese."
- "Violently shakes and 'kills' his stuffed toys."
- "She's fifty pounds and thinks she's a lap dog."

Bette Midler once said, "If somebody makes me laugh, I'm his slave for life." We love people who make us laugh. It's no wonder we love our dogs.

What we take seriously and what we don't says a lot about us. A dog can remind us to let go of the trivial. To let go of the things that don't matter. No one will die because we spilled eggs on the supermarket floor. Unless they slip on them. So laugh. And find a mop.

When I had the joy of experiencing a colonoscopy for the first time, I should have invited my dog to accompany me and lighten things up. I was delighted that this horrific little procedure would be performed an hour from home because I wanted no one who was remotely familiar noticing me. But the first nurse who met me said, "Are you Phil?" She said she had heard me speak somewhere. That I had really helped her through a tough spell. Then she offered me explicit instructions on disrobing and handed me a gown the same size as a French bathing suit. Another nurse arrived to lead me down the hall to the guillotine. She was very kind. She smiled and said, "I love your books." I was looking around for my dignity.

"Knock me out!" I begged.

She laughed.

An hour later, I awoke to discover that she had graciously obliged.

I have yet to meet a couple whose marriage is in trouble, a boss whose staff is out of joint, or the pastor of a church going through a nasty split, who tells me, "You know our problem? We just laughed too much together."

Laughter is the smile of God on a troubled world.

So when you get the chance, go ahead and howl.

11

Nothing Can Steal Your Joy
Until You Give It Permission

Christmas that year was cold. So cold that I did little else but stand and stare through the kitchen window, thinking to myself, *If I keep this up, maybe my wife will let me in.* I mentioned this to the family and everyone laughed.

The season had put us in a jolly mood, and knowing that our favorite Christmas guests were on their way helped. Of all my friends, none was closer to me than Lauren, a TV news cameraman who was married to my wife's sister. A gentle giant, Lauren loved three things: God, family, and a strong cup of coffee—one whiff of which was enough to keep me awake for days.

You don't expect a relative to become a friend, but it's rather nice when it happens, and Lauren quickly became my go-to guy when I was down or just had a good joke to share. A few days before Christmas, he and his wife arrived to stay with us. It was a custom we had enjoyed through the years, but this time they had a new family member along—a border collie named Kelly.

Now border collies are ranked number one in doggy intelligence, but let's face it, they are not right in the head.[1] Acrobatic and extremely energetic, if a border collie is locked indoors as the thermometer plunges and the snow reaches four feet, it will slowly and systematically lose its mind. Needing something to herd, Kelly chose me.

About six o'clock on Kelly's first morning at our house, she nosed our bedroom door open and stood with her face inches from mine. I smelled her breath just before opening my eyes. The eagerness on her face said, "Cows! Get up! They've broken through the fence again!"

I am a night owl. I like to get up at the crack of noon. So I opened one bleary eye and looked at Kelly. All I could think to say was, "I'm gonna call the pound."

She was undeterred. Immovable. "Hey! It's six a.m.! We're late! Get up! Whatcha waitin' for? Let's go!"

I arrived earlier than usual at the breakfast table thanks to the fact that though I had locked Kelly out of our room, she sat outside and softly scratched the door every ten to twelve seconds.

Lauren was in the kitchen, pouring syrupy coffee into manly mugs. And I'll admit, I was a little steamed at the border collie invasion.

"How many border collies does it take to change a lightbulb?" Lauren asked.

"I don't know."

"One," he said, "but he might change the wiring and replace the chandelier too."

"You're not kidding." I told him about my wake-up call, and he apologized. "I'm sorry. I don't know what to do with him."

"No problem," I lied. But it was a problem. By the end of the day, Kelly had followed me everywhere, including the bathroom; engaged in frantic twirling, jumping, and bouncing; chased whatever moved; brought toys, balls, and a plate for me to throw; and then descended our stairs to the basement, where he chewed holes in every available Ping-Pong ball.

Lauren promised to replace them all—the plate too. But I was exasperated and exhausted. This was not the Christmas I had planned.

Mojo took a higher road, ignoring Kelly completely at first and then rolling over and playing submissive. Perhaps she was just hiding her annoyance well, but the dog seemed unflappable. If she could have spoken, she might have said, "Lighten up. You're gonna let a dog steal your Christmas?"

Later that day I threw Kelly a ball and then ran and locked myself in the bedroom. Ten seconds passed. I could hear panting. Then the collie softly scratched at the door.

My wife was standing in the bedroom, grinning. The last few months the seizures had subsided, and hope was returning.

"That miserable dog is driving me crazy," I said, letting out an exasperated whine. "Do you have some poison?"

The grin turned to a laugh, and Ramona had the audacity to say, "Remember—love me, love my dog."

Of course she was right. But it took a little while before I summoned the courage to leave the room and do what I knew to do.

Life with a child or a spouse or a dog gets messy, so you learn to deal with it. And here is what I discovered. Nothing can drive you crazy unless you let it. Nothing can steal your joy, pillage your peace, or loot your happiness until you give it permission. Nothing. Not even a dog. And when that dog is a friend's dog, you wave goodbye to narcissism and say hello to viewing others as more important than yourself. It changes everything.

I was a different boy when I left that room. Kelly could sense it. We took off down the stairs, where I rounded up three tennis balls. We ran up and down the stairs ten times together. I told her to sit, and she did. I panted heavily. She panted lightly.

Coffee has never been my cup of tea, but I said to Lauren, "Hit me with a cup of the strongest java you've got." I tossed it back and shuddered. Then we bundled up and went outside, where Kelly and Mojo chased everything we could throw for them. When we went ice skating, Kelly slid and rolled and barked. The dog lost all three tennis balls in snowdrifts, but it was all right. As I told Lauren, "They're making more of them all the time. You can pick 'em up in stores."

It was one of my favorite Christmases. We still talk about it. We surrounded the table with family and friends, played Dutch Blitz, and sang Christmas carols.

While a border collie named Kelly lay exhausted at our feet.

12

The Best Is Still Out There

I soon became convinced that dogs can hear the opening of a can of tuna from three time zones away. Mojo would be sound asleep in the living room, but within two seconds of the *clink*, she was gazing up at me with expectancy. I learned to leave a little in the bottom, get her to jump a few times in the air, and then zing it across the linoleum. She would lick it around the room until finally lodging it into some cranny, where twenty minutes later she had finished the thing.

Dogs are omnivores. They eat what we eat. With few exceptions, what is good for me is good for my dog. My wife didn't see it this way, so I took to sneaking morsels of the most unlikely offerings beneath the table, where Mojo would entertain almost anything. She did not tolerate tomatoes. Nor lettuce. Nor pickles. But she loved carrots, slowly masticating them and begging for more. Meat she gobbled. Grapes she rolled around her mouth without the heart to finish one. And an hour spent with a bone lodged between her paws was an hour in doggy heaven.

One night I knew I couldn't get away with such sneakiness.

The table was set for seven. The silverware polished as if the maids at Downton Abbey were working overtime. Mom and Dad had arrived after a fifty-foot voyage for an evening meal of glazed chicken and a celebration of the purchase of their brand-new stereo. "I think Noah used the old one on the ark for weather reports," I joked as we sat down. The dog was nestled between my father and me, her hopes set on chicken.

That afternoon I had spent an hour showing Dad how to set the digital clock on the newfangled stereo. His mind was still reeling. Jeffery, who had been admiring the flashing lights and 100-watt speakers said, "Um, Grandpa, you should put this thing in your will. I'd like it. You're not gonna live much longer anyway."

He said this. I wouldn't make this up.

Dad was hard of hearing and replied, "Bill? Who's Bill?"

Mom almost fell off her rocking chair laughing and then recovered enough to say, "Well, Jeffery, the Bible says it's good to remember how short our lives are, 'so that we may be wise.'"

"Surprise?" said Dad. "What surprise?"

We were recounting the conversation while sipping carbonated apple juice when the conversation swung suddenly to the hereafter.

"I don't wanna go to heaven," admitted Jeffery. "All we're gonna do is sit around and talk."

"Where did you hear that?"

"Well, that's all you grownups do. I heard we're just gonna worship God all the time. With a worship band and stuff."

Rachael chimed in. "And there won't be dogs in heaven. If Mojo won't be there, I don't wanna go."

"The Bible doesn't say dogs won't be in heaven," I said. "Just that cats won't." Rachael wrapped me on the knuckles with her spoon.

These questions are virtually impossible to sidestep when you invite aging parents and a dog to cohabit with children. Kids want to know (as did eight people who responded to our survey), will my dog go to heaven?

I had no trouble identifying with Jeffery. In my boyhood, heaven seemed like an extension of church, which, to be honest, was about as exciting as watching jam set. So as the chicken was passed around, I told a joke about an angel who suddenly appeared to a man golfing at Pebble Beach. The angel said, "I can answer any question you want. Go ahead and ask."

The man thought for a moment. "Are there golf courses in heaven?"

The angel replied, "Do you want the good news or the bad news first?"

The man shrugged. "The good news." So the angel told him, "The courses in heaven are so beautiful I can scarcely describe them. There are no green fees, you have your choice of clubs, and electric carts are provided free of charge. All the balls miraculously jump from the rough and float on water so you'll never lose them, and the cups are the size of basketball hoops."

The golfer smiled and asked, "What's the bad news?"

"Well, I booked you for a tee time in five minutes."

Grandma laughed and then shook her head. "Heaven will be amazing," she said.

"Will Mojo be there?" Rachael asked it again.

The dog had a paw on my knee and was scratching a little too hard. "Billy Graham was asked that question by a little girl once," I said, cutting off a dog-sized chunk of meat and wondering what to do with it.

"Phil!" warned my wife.

"What did he say?" asked Rachael.

"He said that if it would make her any happier, her dog would be there."

"Do you really think so?"

"Why not?" asked Grandma.

"I don't know," I said. "I suppose he could make seven little Mojos for you in heaven if it would bring you pleasure."

Dad seemed oblivious to the conversation, perhaps because he had just slipped a bite of chicken from his plate onto the floor while looking around innocently.

"Grandpa," warned Stephen.

Perhaps it is the ultimate tribute to our canine companions that we wish to spend eternity with them. And though I'm no theologian, I've read the Bible. It tells me that God created us and he created our pets. Whatever he has planned for man and beast will be beyond our wildest imaginations.

There is no indication that animals have souls. You don't see them go forward during altar calls, but we know God loves them and had Adam name them.[1] He saved animals from the flood.[2] He scolded Jonah for his reluctance in saving not just the humans in Nineveh but also the animals.[3] Heaven has a vast supply of horses, and animals will be part of the new heaven and new earth.[4] Will they be the exact same dogs we knew and loved? We do not know. But we can know this: In heaven, God is not likely to deprive us of what he delighted us with on earth. And there is great comfort in knowing that the One who knows our every longing loves us and will be there.

I said a somewhat weaker version of this to the kids, and they seemed satisfied enough. And soon, like Grandpa, they were thinking of other things.

"Will there be stereos in heaven?" asked Jeffery.

"Not the kind we have here," I answered. "They'll be far better."

And this is what my child said (I wouldn't make this up either): "Good. Then Grandpa won't be needing his."

Brighten Things for Others
And the Sun Will Shine on You

I know of few families that have faced more challenges than my wife's family. I know of few families that laugh more. As surely as my dog needs to turn around three times before lying down, humans need laughter. It lowers blood pressure, reduces stress, defends against infection, improves memory, and can get you kicked out of seventh-grade health class.[1] Most of these things I know from personal observation.

When Ramona and I began to date, I learned there was a fifty-fifty chance she carried the Huntington's gene. But at twenty-one you're bulletproof. A few years after we married, however, reality set in. Ramona's sisters Miriam and Cynthia began their journey with this fatal genetic disorder that causes mental and physical deterioration. In his thirties, her brother Dennis was already in a nursing home.

One Valentine's Day, after waiting ten months for test results, we discovered that Ramona didn't carry the gene and that our children were clear too. But the seizures continued. My brothers-in-law Bill and Jim, who were nursing invalid wives far too young, became saints to me during those years. They showed me that joy has little to do with where we are and everything to do with believing God won't leave us there. "One day this will all make sense," Bill told me. Somehow he found the perspective to take what life threw his way and say, "We're gonna make it. You just watch."

Sometimes life is hard. For all of us.

The same week we took that family picture with our laughing dog, a letter arrived. I read it flat on my back in our recently mown grass with our laughing dog eyeing me from a few feet away.

Dear Mr. Callaway,

I enjoy your books and your sense of humor. In my early teens laughter was easy. I'm seventeen now, and the joy is gone from my life. How do you live a life of joy?

Blaine Stafford

PS: Here's a cheesy joke for you. There were two peanuts walking down the street. One was a salted.

I set the letter down. Mojo was still eyeing me, lifting a front paw, beseeching me to throw a ball. So I played with her a few minutes, but while my dog ran down a tennis ball, I reflected on my own need to lighten up. Later that night I sat down and wrote a letter to Blaine.

Dear Blaine,

What a great question! Thanks for asking it. I know of no stronger drug to fight stress, tension, discouragement, embarrassment, and fear than laughter. But how do we bring it back? The first thing you need to do is get a dog. Dogs help us laugh. One is sitting at my feet right now. I've just finished a snack, and there's a tiny nibble of cheese still on the plate. She will not rest until I give it to her. I think she wants a reward because today her ferocious ten-minute barking fit saved our entire family from being murdered by the meter reader.

After you get a dog (assuming your parents allow this), you need to find a new joke. I've been peppered before with the one about the peanut being a salted. Try this one. Did you hear about the fire at the circus? It was intense.

Okay, maybe the peanut joke isn't so bad.

First let me say, I've been seventeen. It's not easy. I was skinny and pimply, I had girl trouble, and my car sounded like a cat with hiccups. Seventeen is hard. Fifty is better, but here are a few things I've discovered that can help bring the joy back.

First, realize that joy is a bit like those missing socks from the dryer. You may not find joy by looking for it. It comes from loving God, choosing the best when the worst shows up, and knowing that he is accomplishing amazing things behind the scenes even when life seems messy. (By the way, Blaine, our dog is messy. When I put her food in her dish, I say, "Shall I spread it over the floor for you, or will you knock it over yourself?")

So wake up right each day. If you have to crawl back into bed and start over, that's okay. Go ahead. Take a deep breath. Remember to let it out. Grin. Say a quick prayer of thanks. You woke up in a bed. Breakfast is twenty steps away. Too many people don't have either.

Next, have a wake-up song ready. One that'll focus your mind on things that last forever. Sing it or play it. When we fix our eyes on Jesus, we find there's nothing—not even girl trouble—that the two of us can't handle together today.

Next, say something nice to the first person you see. Maybe it's Mom or Dad or a sibling. Try a compliment about food or clothes or hair. Go slowly at first. The shock may be too much for them. When you leave the house, remember to go MAD (Make A Difference). Like Darth Vader and Luke Skywalker, you'll have opportunity all day to choose the dark or the light. Brighten the world for others, and the sun will shine on you.

People will try to drive you crazy, but you won't let them. Remember everyone on earth is at least just a little bit lonely, so befriend a lonely, uncool person. Make friends who love the right things, who have great attitudes. If you hang out with guys who suck lemons, you'll look really ugly and wrinkly by the time you're my age. Don't blame others. And don't be afraid to get a job flipping burgers. Use half the money to support a needy child through Compassion. It'll change your life. And remember, your teachers aren't so bad. You'll appreciate most of them once you get a boss.

Don't listen to lies grownups tell. Here's one: "You can do anything you set your mind to." Sorry, you can't. Have you watched *American Idol*? But you *can* do anything God wants you to. His script for your life is better than anything you will ever write. So talk to him about it. Find that one thing you love to do. Trust him. Don't rest until he gives you a nibble.

Read the book of Philippians in the Bible. I love learning about joy from a man who was shipwrecked and imprisoned. At night, read the book of Proverbs. You'll find guidance on relationships, money, and the future; you'll learn discernment, confidence, work ethics, and sexual purity. This book will shape your life. And a God-shaped life is a joy-filled life even when tough times show up.

Phil

PS: Don't stop telling jokes. Here's another one for you. What do you call an alligator wearing a vest? An investigator. Actually, your peanut joke is sounding better all the time.

14

Only a Dog Loves You
More than Himself

All my life I have read and repeated heroic dog rescue stories. Not the stories where people rescue dogs, though I find these invigorating, but the ones where dogs rescue people. My pulse surges at headlines like this: "Weiner dog protects owner, stands up to black bear" (I kid you not). Stories abound. Some are legendary.

- A girl out for a walk with her dog sees an abandoned wheelchair and a woman floating in the river. Frantic, she tells her dog Penny, "*Fetch!*" Penny obeys, pulling the drowning woman ashore.

- A boy lost in the mountains is kept from freezing by the warmth of a husky who refuses to leave the boy's side.

- A Texas two-year-old is hurried indoors when the family dog Arf becomes agitated, thus saving the toddler from a twenty-four-inch North American coral snake. Brave Arf is later admitted to a veterinary hospital, where he is photographed for the local newspaper, surrounded by a grateful family, his body covered with snakebites and scratches.

Perhaps there is within all of us a desire to be rescued from where we are.

Mark Bekoff, a professor emeritus at the University of Colorado–Boulder, relates the stirring tale of Norman, a blind Labrador retriever. He was summoned to action by the shrieks of the family's children, who were caught in the current of a foaming river. "Joey had managed to reach the shore, but his sister was struggling, making no headway, and in great distress. Norman jumped straight in and swam after Lisa. When he reached her, she grabbed his tail, and together they headed for safety." I used to make up doggy bravado stories for my children, but none seem more far-fetched than the real thing.

For the most part, dogs actively avoid danger and death, withdraw from high ledges, and are averse to loud noises, rushing rivers, or grizzly bears. Still, there are cases when they seem to overcome instincts for self-preservation and selflessly rush to the aid of other two- and four-legged creatures. Some biologists call into question these anecdotes, asking whether the current merely shifted favorably for blind Norman and Lisa, and if Arf was just doing what dogs do—arfing. Furthermore, they ask why we never read reports of the millions of incidences where dogs abandon shivering hikers or keep right on chasing their tails despite the desperate screams of someone in distress.

As winter vanished and we began to plan for a camping trip by a rushing river, I got to looking at Mojo, wondering if she had the right stuff to be a people rescuer. Believing this question had a measurable, quantitative conclusion, I decided to find out, to test this theory myself with a clever experiment.

A few miles from our house, a lazy creek winds through my favorite golf course. I decided to walk along the edge with Mojo and just fall in as if I'd been shot or overcome. What would she do?

"Hey," I said to my son Jeffery, "come with me. I wanna do something."

He was working on a chemistry assignment and looking for excuses not to be. "Sure. Where we going?"

I outlined plans of my brave experiment, and he let out a snort. "The creek is about this deep." He pointed at his knees and shook his head. "It's gross too. What if people see you? There are golfers out there."

He made some good points. The creek is murky, narrow, and shallow. How could a dog sense danger if there wasn't any? I needed something deeper, more turbulent. "The Bow River," I said. "The best fly-fishing on earth is only hours away. We could go Saturday."

Jeffery smirked. "I don't know. I've seen you swim."

The boy was making more sense all the time. Come to think of it, there was no way I was plunging into the icy waters and entrusting my life to a shih tzu.

And so I decided on a more favorable course of action. I would choose between two homemade scenarios. Both involved feigning an emergency to see how my potential rescue dog would respond. (1) I could put the dog in an adjacent room. My son could pin me under a fallen bookcase, let the dog loose, and see what happened. (2) I could have the dog nearby and simply fake a heart attack right in the comfort of my own house. As the first option involved being pinned beneath a bookshelf, I went with scenario two. This I did in the presence of no one but the dog, believing that if things looked too contrived, the dog's interest would be as phony as my ailment. Furthermore, if my family was present, the dog could be excused for not saving my life.

The only previous heart attack I had faked was a backyard heart attack where I simply lay on the grass with the garden hose running, hoping to see how much my wife loved me. She was hoeing rhododendrons or some such thing and eventually turned and said, "Get up. I need some help here."

This heart attack would be better. Letting out an "Uhhhh!" I clutched my chest with both hands, gasped some more, and collapsed facedown—*clunk!*—hitting the most padded part of the floor, a thick white carpet. I wisely did so in such a way as to leave my head strategically pointed where I could watch my dog. I was motionless, squinting through thin slits. Surely she would inform another human of my plight.

Mojo was perched on the back of the sofa, watching leaves rustle on our laurel leaf willow. I counted to fifty before she sat up, turned her head toward me, and cocked it slightly to the left. *Aha! This may be working.* Hopping from the sofa, she strolled toward me, head down, wagging her tail. *See, she's about to do something!* She pawed my pant leg, climbed aboard, let out a long sigh, turned around twice, and curled up in the small of my back.

I am trying hard to think of a life lesson she taught me in this. Devotion perhaps. If I were dead, the 911 people would at least find her close to me. And the small of my back would be warm. But I suppose all of us long to be rescued. From the mundane, the predictable, the dark places of life.

Maybe I've loved rescue stories from the time I was a child because I read so many in the Bible. David from the giant. Jonah from the fish. Jesus from the grave. There I was told of One who could keep my feet from slipping and rescue me from death.[1] One who would lead me to a place of safety, who would rescue me because he delights in me.[2] One who would rescue me from every evil attack and bring me safely to heaven.[3]

Three minutes after my experiment went awry, I had almost fallen asleep thinking of these things. It was quite comfortable there. I heard Ramona's voice. "You okay?" she asked. I couldn't see her, but I'm certain she was smiling.

"Never better," I said.

15

If Your Dog Is Fat, You May Be Too

Sometimes life gets crazy busy. Mine was. The only exercise I seemed to get was from avoiding deadlines. Carrying things too far. Running stoplights.

With the arrival of our canine houseguest, that began to change. One night Ramona mentioned to me that she thought I could stand a little exercise. "Here's the leash," she said, looking back and forth between me and the dog. Suddenly I realized that if your dog is fat, chances are you could use a little exercise yourself.

The habit formed quickly. Each evening Mojo would fetch me for a daily walk. Too proud to be seen hanging on to the leash of a tiny dog, I enlisted my wife to join me for a ten-minute stroll north of town. It soon became apparent that the dog wasn't just pulling my wife along—it was pulling us together. We usually stretched the walks to twenty minutes or so, up a gentle incline in full view of a prairie sunset. Sometimes we'd stop to watch deer graze along the train tracks, and always we'd talk. When a rabbit scampered past, we'd unleash the hound and laugh at her attempts to track it down.

Some nights after dark, my friend Ron would stop by and say, "Let's go," so I'd harness the pup again and ask Ron to hold the leash.

"No," he declined, "you go ahead."

"Before our dog came along," I told him, "the only time I got exercise was when my wife hid the remote."

We were already puffing like smokers on a treadmill, trying to keep up with this little dog.

"Maybe I should get one," said Ron, a decidedly non-dog guy.

Ten years earlier a physician frowned as he listened to Ron's heart. Like me, my friend loves triple-decker cappuccino cheesecake smothered in chocolate sauce, but the doctor ordered him to change his eating habits and get more exercise or he'd be staring down the barrel of a heart attack ten years down the road.

Six months ago the doctor's prediction came true. Ron had a massive heart attack at forty-three.

Location is everything with heart attacks. Just ask Ron. He was fifty yards from a fully staffed ambulance at the time. A cardiologist happened to be walking by. Apparently God had more for Ron to do down here.

His brush with death brought some changes to his life. Our little walking habit was one of those changes.

"Owning a dog can add years to your life, you know."

"Say what?" wheezed Ron.

I told him about studies indicating that, on average, dog owners enjoy longer life spans and improved cardiovascular fitness, and they tend not to suffer as often from depression, high blood pressure, and loneliness.

"There's this study of Chinese women that showed there were fewer doctor visits and less use of sick days at work when a dog was present in the home."

"But I'm not a Chinese woman," said Ron.

I told him that Australian dog owners use free government health services less, and German pet owners spend one-third fewer nights hospitalized than their petless peers.

"Where did you hear this?"

"I read it online, so it must be true."

My words were increasingly punctuated with labored breathing, so I stopped and said, "You're almost a senior, you know. Seniors who care for dogs have more purpose than those who don't." I mentioned a small-scale study of elderly people hospitalized for coronary ailments. Within a year, eleven of the twenty-nine patients without pets passed away, compared to only three of the fifty-two owning a pet.

"You're making that up."

"No I'm not. These animals are employees at hospitals now. Schools, prisons, nursing homes, psychiatric wards," I said. "You'll find them in waiting rooms. They help with irritation, pain, and emotional distress. They help military vets with post-traumatic stress disorder. Stress hormones drop for autistic children when a dog joins the family."

I sounded like a used-car salesman. "They're the closest thing you can have to grandchildren at your age, Ron. They make you laugh. They listen well. They get you to walk in better places than shopping malls. They're always overjoyed to see you. You can blame stuff on them. They help you meet new people. And no one wants them in five-star hotels, so you save money."

We'd come full circle back to my house, and Ron was looking down at my dog. "How much do you want for her?" he asked.

"Twenty bucks?"

"Potty trained?"

"Yep."

"I'll think about it."

"I'll throw in a year's supply of dog food. But seriously, one lady I know who suffers from depression says she's seen an improvement since getting a small dog. Pretty cool."

I didn't tell him he was looking at the small dog or that the "lady" was me. Among other things, depression was having a hard time out-living a daily five-mile hike.

Along about ten p.m. I was removing Mojo's collar when the door-bell rang. Our neighbor Irene was stopping by with her daughter Cassandra. They had discovered some months ago that one doesn't need to own a dog to experience the health benefits. "May we rent your dog?" Cassandra laughed. The evening walks were helping her mom battle kidney disease as they awaited news of a possible transplant.[1]

"Of course you can," I said, pulling Mojo's collar back on. "That'll be two bucks."

The dog was bringing a fitness revolution to the entire neighborhood. She would sleep well tonight.

16

The Good Life Is Right in Front of Us

When We Stop Wanting a Better One

Life with a chronic slobbering optimist was not always rosy. There were mornings when I didn't want to be drooled on by a dog who was perky, lively, and alert, a dog whose life seemed to be a never-ending string of amazing, stupendous, wonderful, and awesome. Though my bouts with depression were lifting, I still had my days. And on those days I felt like locking Mojo in another room so I could mope about undisturbed.

The pup reminded me of my friend James. He and his dog Bella were good walking companions for us. Bella was a shy and quiet breed, but James made up for it. Lately he had been barking a little too loudly I thought. James and his bride Anne were about to escape on a month-long vacation, and he couldn't stop reminding me that I was going nowhere. Finally they found someone to take Bella and boarded a flight for Europe. I was happy for them. I really was. He's a college professor, so he works hard six or seven months a year. But for me, deadlines were looming. The day he left our sewer backed up. Then we endured days of rain. It had me looking around for an ark.

Then the barking began. Which is to say that James began sending irritating little email updates describing how magnificent and fantastic things were in his neck of the world.

> Beautiful sunny day for walking around Rome. Hung out at the Coliseum and the Forum. Quite a city. Think I got a sunburn. Have a great day!

As I read that first email and pondered an appropriate response, Mojo was dozing on the floor beside me without a care in the world. Not only did I envy James, I envied our little hound. But this didn't stop me from pushing Reply and writing back.

> That sounds fantastic, James! I'm envious but glad for you. Give thanks for that sunburn. I got a rain burn today. Take care.

I heard nothing but silence for two days. Then he launched his second volley.

> The sun has not stopped shining here. My second cousin works at the Vatican library, so he invited us to a garden party. Quite spectacular. Hope all is going well. Grace and peace, James.

I let it sit a few days, typed the following, and hit Send.

> So! Garden party at the Vatican, huh? Ramona and I had a garden party last night. The rain stopped long enough for us to weed our garden. Did you snap any pictures? Was the pope there? Did he let you try on his hat? I'm glad your second cousin works at the Vatican library. I have some second cousins who are finally out of prison. Our sewer backed up again today, so a crew comes tomorrow to dig up our driveway. Better go—my daughter just brought her car over. Somebody ran into her, and the passenger side doors won't open. Grace but not necessarily peace, Phil.

In no time this arrived.

> We had a great laugh reading your email. You should write comedy! Yesterday we visited the Sistine Chapel, saw Michelangelo's great frescos on the ceiling, ate some incredible pizza, and enjoyed more blue sky. Today we hopped a train to Venice. The Grand Canal. Gondolas. More blue sky. An evening stroll in San Marco square.

I responded immediately.

> We are sorry, your email was blocked due to excessive gloating. Please send a dismal report should you encounter one.

Not to be outdone, James continued.

> Dear St. Phil, As much as I would like to report that things are going badly, I cannot. We are dining like royalty. Food is flowing on an endless conveyer belt. Maybe tomorrow will be awful and I can cheer you up with the details. James.

I couldn't type fast enough.

> Sadly, your email came through in German. I think it instructed me to put your house up for sale. You'll be pleased to know interested parties are walking through it now. I just got the bill from the sewer repair guys. Almost had a conniption, which is a rare thing. Our parents had conniptions, but you don't hear about them much anymore. Travel safe. Your envious buddy, Phil.

I read our exchange to my wife, and we enjoyed a good laugh. But veiled behind a sense of humor was my own discontent. Mojo was contentedly gnawing a bone at my feet. She didn't seem to get all worked up comparing schedules and hairdos and vacations and weather patterns. Puppies don't compare. Sure, they sniff to find out what another dog has been up to, but schnauzers don't mope about wishing they were wolfhounds. Nail-polish sales are very low in the dog world (except among poodle owners). We humans compare our animals, our cars, our salaries. And comparison is the mother of all stress inducers.

If Mojo could have spoken, she might have said, "The good life is right in front of us—when we stop wanting a better one."

With James due home in a week, I looked at that dog and knew exactly what to do. I knew that gratitude was the most direct route to contentment, so I gave thanks to God for all he'd given me. I knew contagious joy evaporates as we nurse the sin of comparison, so I determined to rejoice with those who rejoice, to celebrate the successes of others. And I sent another email inviting James and Anne to a Welcome Back to the Rain Pizza Party, where they could show us photos of their trip.

A friend was having a garden party. I would stop having a pity party.

17

Some Things Are Worth Chasing, Some Are Not

Our neighbors a few doors to the north had two cats, Prince Caspian and Chairman Meow. Both were expert mousers. Aside from the odd mouse carcass on our porch, we appreciated their efforts to keep our neighborhood rodent-free. Mojo, however, was not a fan. She loved to chase cats down the street and return in triumph. But one day, Chairman Meow was sitting in our flower bed thinking to himself, *Hey, I'm twice the size of this little rat.* And from then on he determined to stand his ground.

The world shifted for Mojo that day. She took off fast after Mr. Meow—and thudded into an immovable object. Chasing a sixteen-pound cat was like pursuing a parked car. Mojo just sat there stunned, thinking, *Some things are worth chasing, some are not.*

My neighbor Joel and I laughed about this little incident. I think he was secretly proud of his cat. I was proud of my dog. He was learning to respect a cat's right to be a cat. He does not necessarily approve, admire, or assuage them. But increasingly he is becoming a dog of peace and tranquility.

We were standing before Joel's open garage at the time, and I had never seen the inside of it before. I said, "Whoa, you should open a dollar store."

Now Joel was a self-admitted hoarder. Like one out of every four double-garage owners, Joel owned vehicles that had never seen the inside of his garage. Instead he had crammed it with stuff. Old tax returns. Newspapers. Collectibles. His children's old toys. His parents' old belongings.

I had the tendency myself. My shed and study were miniature versions of Joel's garage. I had a possession obsession. For years I had cherished and accumulated stuff, once scolding my mother for unwisely ditching childhood toys and baseball cards that were surely worth a mint.

I loved to stroll through flea markets for a catalog of hoardable objects—varsity letter jackets, 8-track tapes, rotary phones, typewriters, old ties and cowboy boots, butterflies pinned to cardboard and framed...

Joel and I talked about our animals and then exchanged collector's stories. A G.I. Joe Mickey Mouse Cobra Commander, originally 50 cents, was now worth $300. The Royal Blue Beanie Baby, once $10, was now $3000.

"You don't have one of those Star Wars Ewok Combat sets, do you?"

"No."

"It sold for $17 in 1984. You can get $6000 for it now. Unless you opened the box."

Joel laughed and shook his head.

Mojo sat at my feet. The embarrassment of being humbled by a cat had worn off. And I suddenly realized that apart from dragging the odd bone home, this dog requires nothing more than food and shelter to live her happy life.

It's quite a contrast from the average North American. Our households contain on average 300,000 items, from pens to pants to paper clips. American children make up 3.7 percent of children on the planet but cling to 47 percent of all its toys and children's books.[1]

So why this need to hoard? According to experts, stuff helps us keep up with the Joneses and offers a sense of security and a connection to the past—to the people we love. But 50 percent of hoarders suffer from major depression, and studying my dog that day, I knew I needed to do something.[2]

Starting with the basement, I tossed anything that was busted, redundant, or useless. I kept things that were beautiful, meaningful, or useful. I wasn't ready to have my wife help me yet, but unstuffing felt so good. An old Irish proverb says, "A dog owns nothing but is seldom dissatisfied."

It would take time, but gradually I learned to do without any media that I thought I couldn't do without. And most of the things I did not need. And as many things as possible that needed to be dusted. I learned to do without most new gadgets that were built to break and be updated and complicate my life. And anything I was buying to impress others.

Like my dog, I began learning to enjoy things without owning them. They gave me just as much pleasure. Sometimes more. Like my dog, I began learning to put less stock in titles, status, and position, and I found I had more time for family, friends, and God.

Increasingly the clothes in my closet fit me. I felt less overwhelmed and more grateful.

Collecting hadn't just cluttered my home—it had cluttered my life and my mind. I hadn't just held on to stuff but also to resentments and regrets. Such a turnaround takes years, but walking to the shed with a tiny dog nipping at my heels, I knew I was heading in the right direction.

18

Dogs Have No Need to Impress, Acquire, or Tweet

As another summer came and went, my schedule grew out of control. The air miles mounted, but I had no time to redeem them. Mojo had taken to crawling into my suitcase as I was packing and just looking at me with mournful eyes. Fatigue became an ever-present reality. Books with stress tests only reminded me that most of the leading stressors were pressing in on us. I was using Pepto-Bismol as gravy. The only time I stopped to smell the roses was when I crashed into a flower shop.

Of our surveyed dog owners, 57 percent agreed that their dogs provide stress relief. For some, this meant going for walks. Others said their dogs reminded them of the need to laugh more often or to sit still sometimes.

For me, this dog was to provide stress relief in tandem with an unusual object—the family mirror. Perhaps more than any common household item, the mirror shows us the difference between humans and dogs. I tiptoed up behind Mojo one morning while she was facing in the general direction of a floor-length mirror, and she somehow saw my approaching form in the mirror and turned around. After extensive testing on our canine companions, experts tell us that dogs sometimes appear as though they are examining another animal and in some cases, like the one above, even use mirrors to gather information. But dogs never study themselves in the mirror.

We humans have mirrors in our entryways, hallways, bathrooms, cars, and purses. We use them to select a suit, apply makeup, and rid ourselves of mango strings between our teeth. But a dog has never been known to sit before a mirror yipping about a bad haircut or wishing the tip of their tail was black. Dogs seem to have little concept of their size or shortcomings. Pride, it could be said, is in short supply in man's best friend.

Twice I tested this theory myself, holding Mojo in front of the mirror. Both times she glanced at it briefly and then turned away, disinterested.

And it hit me. If I'm truly honest, I must admit that pride lurks at the heart of so much of my stress. It certainly accounts for 93 percent of social media's lure. One night my wife asked, "Why do you post, blog, and tweet almost every day?"

I said something like, "That I might continue to be a blessing to thousands of people," and I'd like to think there was a measure of truth in my attempt at humor. But the real truth is, it's about me. My name, my fame.

After returning from a quiet mountain retreat in a place too remote for cell coverage, I thought, *I haven't written anything to my poor "followers" for three days! What will they think? Are they okay? Are they concerned? Worried? Disappointed? Or worse, have they forgotten I exist?* People I had never met and who will not show up at my funeral had become more important than I cared to admit. Sometimes I was working late to please them, ignoring those who love me most.

Of all the problems contributing to my stress and busyness, I came to see that the most pervasive was pride. Looking in the mirror I thought, *Dogs have no need to Twitter.*

Before long my dog put its paw on other areas of my life that could use a tune-up.

Weary and burned out, I was lying on the carpet one night. As I scratched Mojo's ears I realized I had begun to envy my dog's schedule. As George Carlin asked, "What does a dog do on his day off? He can't lie around. That's his job."

A day in the life of a dog consists of very few formal appointments. Along about dinnertime each day there was a bark at our door. It was Mojo's sniff-mate Sidney, inviting her out to play. But that was all she had on the calendar. Here was Mojo's morning schedule.

8:00 a.m.	Awake. Stretch. Go crazy. Have breakfast.
9:00 a.m.	Nap.
10:00 a.m.	Awake. Stretch. Go crazy. Think of food.
10:05 a.m.	Sniff around. Roll in stuff.
11:00 a.m.	Scratch. Chew on stuff. Bark at nothing. Yawn. Nap.
11:15 a.m.	Must find bones. Must hide bones in closet, behind sofa pillow, in my master's shoe.
12:00 p.m.	Go crazy. Have lunch.

Dogs do not attend performance evaluations, inform others of how busy they are, or rush about trying to please everyone. A dog rarely says yes to committee appointments. Or no to a nap or evening stroll.

On one of those walks, my friend Ron, who travels the world as a photographer, was describing to me the busyness of his travel schedule. "Why am I doing so much?" he asked.

"Because you're addicted to approval," I said.

He stopped and grinned. "I think you're right. How did you know?"

"Because I am too," I laughed.

And here's what I said to him. It was the same unscripted comment I used while speaking to several hundred pastors, most of whom were weary beyond consolation: "God will do fine without you. But your wife won't. Let's covenant together to slow down. There's nothing godly about a nervous breakdown."

There was a popping sound in the room as if someone pulled a cork from a bottle. At first a few likely thought of branding me a heretic and grabbing some matches, but the more it sunk in, the more we all knew it was true.

Dogs have no need to perform. They enter life helpless and penniless. So do we. But a dog does not spend his entire life acquiring possessions so he can impress others and leave stuff behind for those who didn't earn it. He may bury the odd bone for later—usually forgetting its whereabouts—but you will never see a dog featured on a show about hoarders.

Dogs have no need to acquire. And what does a dog need? To eat and sleep. To find a tree or a fire hydrant. A dog needs to love and be loved. To sit at the feet of his master.

I am not suggesting laziness in any form. But the older I get, the more I have come to see that it's a great gift to perform meaningful work, serve others, show mercy, and live generously. But I can do this and miss the most important thing—sitting at the feet of Jesus. When I stop looking in the mirror and take time to do this, I find that he is the only one strong enough to rescue me from the pull of busyness.

Fatigue and stress were unavoidable. Chaos seemed ever-present. But I had to admit that at the root of it all was pride. And the way to start hacking at that root was to develop a habit of daily time with God, in the Bible, and in prayer.

I think my dog would agree. Sometimes we need to turn around three times and lie down at the feet of our master.

19

People Like People
Who Like People

One Sunday afternoon, my son Jeffery was systematically driving the dog crazy. Putting Scotch tape on her fur. Jumping out at her just to see her jump. Less than thrilled by his antics, I asked him to stop or go to his room until he was seventeen. Dogs, I told him, make us laugh, but the idea of a prank is lost on them. "You're likely taking five years off her life, and she won't trust you," I said.

I made a mistake then. I told Jeffery about pranks we used to play on humans. Back before we could afford television, pranks were the meat and potatoes of our entertainment diet. My mother was the first one I knew to play pranks that kept us all on our toes.

One night she short-sheeted my bed, which was a staple for any self-respecting prankster. I later learned how she did it, folding the sheet upward and tucking it in. When I crawled into bed, my entire world was thrown into confusion. I couldn't get in. My legs couldn't get past the three-foot mark, and I was forced to pull the bed apart and remake it myself. "*Dad!*" I yelled. But it was my mom.

Another bedtime prankster lurked in our house. One night I knelt beside my bed and, as my mother had instructed me to do, read the Bible. If I recall correctly, the verse that jumped out at me was, "Be ye kind one to another." After closing the book and saying a quick prayer, I attempted to jump into my pajamas, only to discover that someone had taped the bottoms shut. I fell headlong into a bookcase. "Tim!" I yelled. But it was my sister Ruth.

Other marvelous pranks I encountered through the years included the spreading of a layer of cream cheese over the target's deodorant.

Putting powdered Kool-Aid inside a showerhead. Filling a hair dryer with talcum powder. Tying the infamous rubber band around the kitchen sink spray nozzle just before your sister does the dishes. And gluing all twelve eggs into a carton.

Jeffery snickered as I admitted these things, and I followed them with a warning. "Don't you dare play one more single prank on that dog or else."

"I promise."

"Your brother gave Mojo a hot pepper when she was just a pup."

His eyes widened. "What did she do?"

"Scratched at her face a lot. I gave her some milk. It's the only time she's had it. And it was the last time Stephen did that. I need you to promise you'll be kind to the dog."

He promised.

"You have time for one more story?"

"Sure."

I told him of Greg Benson of Glendale, California, an experienced prankster, who decided to use his pranking abilities for good. One day, Greg and his team of fellow pranksters descended on the Ascencia Homeless Shelter and turned it into a five-star restaurant. When the usual patrons entered the shelter, they were wide-eyed to find live classical music, a custom-made menu, and waiters in black ties serving filet mignon and creamy desserts. To top it all off, Benson and his team donated $5000 to the shelter.

"I've noticed that you've been eager to walk the dog lately. That's great."

"No problem," he said.

"I saw you downtown this afternoon."

"You did?"

"Every girl in town stopped to talk with you. It was like you were Matthew McConaughey."

"Why do girls like a guy with a dog?"

Rachael was coming through the room and heard his question. "A dog is a chick magnet," she said. "It's cute. And a guy with a dog is a guy who cares. If he treats a dog nice, maybe he'll treat me nice. A guy who cares will be good with kids."

"You'll be kind to the dog too, won't you?"

He promised that he would.

His older brother, Stephen, overheard the conversation and said from the next room, "Here, Mojo. Let's go for a walk."

The very next week in a long grocery store self-checkout line, I had a chance to practice what I preach.

In front of me was an older man in obvious discomfort.

"Are you okay?" I asked.

"It's the chemo and radiation," he said. "I'm a little unsteady."

I relieved him of his shopping items (steak and bananas) and put them in my cart. "Can you lean on the cart?" I asked. "Does that help?"

"Yes. Thanks."

"I'm sorry about the chemo. It's nasty."

Keith told me of the battle with leukemia and how his daughter wasn't taking it so well. When we reached the front of the line, he was still a little woozy, so I accompanied him to the checkout. I knew what I should do, but I admit I thought of avoiding it. After beeping his items through I said, "Let's try my card. See if it works."

"What?" he asked. "Why?"

"Because I didn't get you anything last Christmas."

He laughed and shook his head.

"A childhood friend of mine battled cancer, Keith. He had an amazing faith in Jesus, and that has made all the difference. I can't wait to see him in heaven one day. Tell me I'll see you there too?"

"Yes," he answered, "you will."

Jeffery was getting along better with Mojo a week later, judging from the number of walks the two were taking and how quickly the dog climbed onto his lap. I think the boy would agree that simple acts of kindness can make friends, melt hearts, and change minds. Simple acts of kindness can transform lousy days into bright ones and leave lasting memory marks. Nothing speaks louder than a kind word. Nothing is stronger than a helping hand.

When my new friend Keith found out I followed Jesus, he admitted that his best experiences weren't with such people. I told him I was sorry about that. "They should be," I said. I follow one who, in the ultimate act of kindness, loved me enough to die for me. Setting aside my chintziness to buy steak and bananas should come more easily. I've seen kind words to a harried parent make their week. I've seen kind thoughts in a short note hang on a fridge for years.

I remember thinking about my need to do more of this as I made the mistake of turning on our kitchen tap.

You Don't Have to Understand to Be Happy

Nothing seemed to frighten this tiny hound with the exception of two things. The first was our smoke detector. To my children the smoke detector merely meant that Dad was cooking supper, but to my dog it meant her entire world was caving in. The high-pitched shriek made her frantic. She clamored for the door, and if we let her escape, she took off down the street, tail limp, ears slicked backward. A stranger two blocks away brought her home the first time it happened and said, "Is this your dog?" Mojo was terrified, shaking like a caterpillar caught in a restaurant salad.

After the second burnt-toast catastrophe, she stopped a few hundred feet away and then crept back toward the house, pacing the neighbor's yard, surveying our bungalow like a kid who won't go near the closet at night.

Finally, she pawed at my parents' door. Dad opened it, and Mojo quickly disappeared into their suite. I tapped on the door and was surprised to find that Mojo had jumped up on Dad's lap and wouldn't move. Dad was actually scratching her back and offering words of comfort to the traumatized dog as she grinned up at him past crooked teeth. Her fear would become the very thing that endeared her to my father.

A few months earlier, he had turned eighty-one, and that Saturday for the first time ever, he confided in me that he had been experiencing his share of fear. Doubt too.

"Do *you* ever doubt?" Dad looked down at the woolly little dog on his lap, but he was asking me.

The words took me by surprise. Doubt? Are you kidding me? My dad? Doubt? The man who was part Scotch and part ginger ale until he met Jesus? The one who experienced a radical transformation and then studied the Bible and served God for fifty years? Surely you don't have doubts when this is your story. Perhaps there was more of Thomas in him than I thought.

Mom sat in her rocking chair knitting slippers for one of the grandchildren. "Growing old ain't for kids," she said without looking up. "This is the hardest chapter."

Dad repeated his question.

"Yes," I stammered, "I sure do. Every thinking Christian faces doubts, don't they?"

Dad seemed more cheerful at the thought of not being alone in this. But as we talked, I realized that his doubts had little to do with issues related to premillennialism or transubstantiation. They had to do with doubting the love of God. Perhaps these were related to the fact that his mom died when he was a baby and he was raised by an odd assortment of relatives, something that left him wounded and withdrawn at times.

"We weren't supposed to doubt in our church," he said, scratching Mojo's ears. "When I do, I feel like…" Dad's voice trailed off.

"Like you're disqualified?"

He blinked and looked at me. "Yes."

"John the Baptist doubted, you know." Who was I to tell Dad this? He had served God as a Christian bookstore manager and then a minister. He'd preached sermons on John the Baptist. He knew answers to hard questions. Knew that a faith challenged by doubt is often stronger in the end. Knew to replace such thoughts with things that are true and good. Maybe that's why there was a Bible open beside his recliner. And one beside his bed. He led an active prayer life. He had read the finest books giving reason to his faith. He modeled obedience to the voice of God.

Perhaps he needed something more.

That night my wife invited my parents to join us for a barbecue on the back deck. Following dessert, the grandkids grabbed a football. And Mojo hopped up on Grandpa's lap once again. He didn't seem to mind. "Why is she shaking?" he asked. I knew immediately. Weather forecasters be warned, this dog could detect an incoming storm with startling accuracy.

Sure enough, to the west, dark clouds had peeked over the horizon. Minutes later they growled softly, and then they began a slow march toward us across the broad prairie sky. Long before the rumbling began, Mojo had started panting and then shaking as if she had one paw in a light socket. Smoke detectors were bad enough. This was worse.

Inside we went. The kids continued tossing the football near my wife's collection of knickknacks. The pup plunged beneath some furniture. Dad pulled her out and sat her on his lap.

Whispering something to the dog, he patted her Ewok head reassuringly. Small beads of hail were bouncing off the roof now, and an irrational fear had gripped her tiny body. She trembled. She shook. She wouldn't be comforted.[1]

For the first time ever, Dad put his arms around the dog and pulled her close. "I've got you," I heard him say. "Don't worry. The storm can't get you. It's gonna be okay."

I suppose I could have preached a sermon about how God has his arms around us in the storm. That we can trust him entirely. But I didn't need to. I could have told Dad that one of the things this dog has taught me is that we don't have to understand everything to be happy. That we must never stop learning, but we must have the humility to realize that we will never know or understand everything, including things we'd love to know and understand.

I'm sure this dog has questions about the storm. Or questions like, "Why did they call it 'getting me fixed' when afterward it doesn't work anymore?" I'm sure this dog is thoroughly confused by many of my activities, but still she loves me. To her I am a source of protection and food. I hold the keys to the outside kingdom of trees and dirt and all things wonderful. I keep her from things she'd like. Garbage cans. Highways. Cars. Bad food. She doesn't understand, but that's okay.

I'm not sure if she always views me as kind and generous or if she thinks I know what's best for her. Still she loves me.

If I'm honest, I feel a little like this when it comes to my view of God. So much I don't understand. And yet I must admit that a God I can understand would be too small a God to worship.

"Blessed are those who have not seen but still believe," said Jesus.

And I believe.

As the hail stopped and the storm blew over, Dad seemed to relax his hold on the dog. "This dog is a blessing," I heard him say. I would hear those words dozens of times in the days and years to come. I'm sure the doubts lingered, but for now a small dog managed to remind him that someone bigger had his arms around us. It would be okay.

We All Walk with a Limp

I am sometimes asked the difference between a comedian and a humorist. "About three thousand bucks," I say. Age tends to turn a stand-up comic into a sit-down comic, and difficulty tends to turn a comic into a humorist—someone who loves humor but has found that life hurts sometimes and it's okay to talk about that too.

During the summer of Mojo's third year, I finally decided to move my office to our house, packing books and cords and cartoon calendars home. Ramona's seizures had worsened, so I wanted to be there and help out where I could. I discovered quickly that for a guy, just paying attention to your children for long periods of time—like thirty seconds—is hard work. Making sandwiches requires coordination and foresight. Crafting meals that are warm when served and contain actual vegetable particles is heroic. You help with homework. You do something called laundry. And you deal with teachers who say your child's homework has been a mess since you started helping. These things take wisdom and self-restraint.

Each seizure came unexpectedly, of course, throwing Ramona to the floor or the bed or the sofa. Recovery took time and patience, and uncertainty was our new normal. More specialists tried to help. Nothing worked. She couldn't drive, so I added chauffeur to my titles of nurse, chef, and encourager. At first I took to these titles with fervor. But the cancer of resentment, in remission for a time, was back. Despite the proliferation of sermons I preached to myself while doing menial tasks, the questions came. *What about* my *needs? Don't* I *deserve a break?*

Along about then the dog seemed to switch allegiances. Whenever Ramona sat down, Mojo hopped up beside her, curled up on her lap, or rested her head on a knee. Wherever her mistress went, the dog followed—sometimes inches behind her. "She's making me nervous," Ramona laughed.

I've since read that dogs who live in homes with epileptics can be reasonably good predictors of seizures. Two separate studies report that dogs whimpered, stood nearby, licked the person's hands or face, or moved protectively on behalf of the patient. In one case, just before a seizure, a dog blocked a child's access to a staircase. In another, the dog sat on a child's chest, presumably to keep him from harming himself.

Though Mojo didn't show such acuity, she did stay close to Ramona during the horrific episodes and afterward as well. She could do little but be there. Like me, I suppose.

One day an acquaintance who knew our story took me aside and asked, "Why don't you put her in a home and get on with life?"[1] I couldn't think of a fitting response. At first I wanted to smite him with a blunt object. But over the next few days his words began to fester. Maybe he had a point.

And then I watched my dog.

Watched her turn her eyes upward, wondering how her mistress was doing.

Mojo's unwavering loyalty and commitment only cemented itself in tough times.

My dog taught me to stay.

They say that writers are too self-centered to be lonely. But you don't have to be a writer for selfishness to be your besetting sin. Few things bring it out in me more than my marriage. The Christian teaching on marriage is not an easy one: I am to love my wife as Jesus loves the church, ready to lay my life down for her.[2] This dog taught me that kind of commitment. You stay because it's the right thing to do. You stay when hope seems gone. You stay because happiness is something you won't catch by chasing it, but by chasing other things. Obedience. Integrity. Serving others.

The truly great relationships are those that find light in dark places, so we scrawled the word "hope" on paper, stuck it to the fridge, and went looking for it. We began to talk with specialists, accept reasonable advice, and solicit the prayers of praying friends—including ministers who cared and prayed too. We turned to the Bible. Psalm 42 became a favorite: "Why am I discouraged? Why is my heart so sad? I will put my hope in God! I will yet praise him—my Savior and my God!" We found that hope opens doors despair has slammed shut. Hope looks for the good instead of harping on all that's wrong. Like the sun, hope casts shadows behind us as we move toward it.

Most days we walked this eager dog on the path that wanders north out of town, and I began to notice that Mojo had developed an angled gait that helped our walks take longer.

I suppose any relationship worth its salt has a limp to it. But with time, that limp can become the very thing that endears us to one another. The more I decided to stay, the more I came to respect my wife for the fighter she is. She came to love me too, warts and all. Ask her, and she'll assure you that my oddities and shortcomings have become part of the amusing package that she has accepted, forgiven, and chosen not to dwell on. It's the same for me. I learned to curl up beside her while the seizures played out. To talk to her and sing and pray. Just to be there.

Patience and acceptance are among a dog's best gifts to us, and we can afford to give them too.

I learned to say, "Good girl" more often. To encourage. To put my head on her lap and watch a movie of her choosing. I learned to stop nagging about money. To have more fun.

She learned to say, "Good boy" sometimes. That I responded well to food. In fact, the promise of a sandwich in an hour was all the incentive I needed to mow the grass.

I once asked a famous preacher how he stayed married forty-two years. He said two things—repentance and forgiveness. Amen. I think I would add another—commitment.

One of the most common commands we issue to our dogs is "Stay!"

I have learned to stay too, knowing it's the right thing, believing that the worse always comes before the better.

Humility Is like Underwear
Wear It, Don't Show It

On any given day at least three cats pass through our yard, sometimes dragging mouse parts, sometimes lingering about our tomato plants. In the interest of world peace and goodwill among neighbors, an unwritten rule states that we be kind to one another's animals and not write demeaning things if one of us is an author.

We do not say things to the cats like, "I see you have no leash. We put our dog on a leash because we want to keep her."

When a neighbor's cat climbed a telephone pole just off our property, my son admitted that it may have had something to do with the fact that he had chased it with a broom. I told him he must inform the owner of the cat's whereabouts, to which he replied, "You don't own a cat, they own you," which may have been true but didn't get him off the hook.

If a dog can teach us about life, love, and God, surely a cat can too. At least this was my neighbor John's theory, which he expounded as we stood beneath the telephone pole, scratching our heads and gazing up at the frightened cat. It was not John's cat, but another neighbor's who would be along momentarily, we were certain. "What can we learn from cats?" John asked. It was a fair question, and we tried to figure out the answer.

"We can learn from their mistakes," I said. "There are better places to hide than atop thirty-foot, branchless trees."

"I read somewhere that five hundred million birds are killed each year by cats in the United States," John said.

"That should teach us to be kinder."

The cat looked a lot calmer than I would have atop that pole.

"They teach us to rest. Cats nap without ceasing. Up to twenty hours a day, I'm told."

"But sloth is not a virtue," said John.

I told him that a cat can teach us to spend time with people when they're working. To sprawl across their laps, walk on their keyboards, knock an item off their desk, and then pounce on it. "If you watch a cat and imitate it, you may find yourself sneaking up behind your wife and just grabbing her by the socks. Or waking her in the middle of the night and staring at her, three inches from her face."

Another neighbor arrived with a tall ladder and wondered how we could be laughing when a cat was in danger of dying.

We explained. And added one more mind to brainstorm on things we can learn from our feline friends.

We can learn to keep ourselves clean. To soak in the sun. To explore. To enjoy the view more often. A cat teaches us that the world is filled with adventure, so sit up and take notice. Stretch after a nap. And better yet, stretch our minds, learn something new. Cats seem to be reasonably good listeners. That's an admirable trait to have. "So we shouldn't get up while a friend is talking and just walk from the room," I added.

We can appreciate the way cats don't worry so much about what others think. They don't lie awake wondering if they impressed or offended anyone that day. We can appreciate the fearlessness of kittens—they see themselves as lions. They embrace life and independence and companionship too. They show appreciation with a purr. Cats rarely pick favorites. They'll share their time with anyone—or ignore everyone equally.

"I once watched a cat fall asleep, literally," said John. "He fell four feet from a dresser while snoozing, landed on the floor, bounced, and was fine."

"I need to relax more," I said, "though you won't find me up on a dresser."

We craned our necks upward and said together, "Yikes."

The animal was staring at us as if we were its loyal subjects.

We weren't the first men to contemplate cats. In 1955, C.S. Lewis wrote to a friend, "We were talking about cats and dogs the other day and decided that both have consciences but the dog, being an honest, humble person, always has a bad one, but the cat is a Pharisee and always has a good one. When he sits and stares you out of countenance he is thanking God that he is not as these dogs, or these humans, or even as these other cats!"

Lewis was, of course, referring to Jesus's story of two men praying. One was a Pharisee, the other a despised tax collector. The Pharisee prayed, "Thank you, God, that I'm not a sinner like everyone else!" But the tax collector wouldn't even lift his eyes to heaven as he prayed, "O God, be merciful to me, a sinner." Jesus said, "I tell you, this sinner, not the Pharisee, returned home justified before God. Those who exalt themselves will be humbled, and those who humble themselves will be exalted."[1]

A dog is a humble person. A cat would never even hope to be accused of such a thing.

Perhaps the best lesson I learned from the neighbor's cat that day was to be a little more doglike, to stop judging others, to look at things from different angles, gain a new perspective sometimes.

When Joanne, the flustered cat owner, finally arrived, we had just leaned the ladder against the pole. It was a 20-foot ladder, so I'm not sure what we were hoping for.

Joanne was in an understandable huff, phoning her husband, when we heard a scratching noise followed by a soft thud. We still don't know how, but the cat managed to come down the way she went up. My son and the broom were nowhere to be seen. The cat was fine.

Nothing Is Often a Very Clever Thing to Say

have witnessed a handful of miracles in my life. Topping the list is the remarkable turnaround in my wife's health. A new doctor prescribed a simple antiseizure medication the others had overlooked, and in no time she was waking up beside the most thankful guy alive.

But improved health is not necessarily the prescription for a happy marriage, and I know of few guys who have committed more fatal relational errors than someone whose whiskers I shave each morning. I could be critical, demanding, and irritating—all by breakfast time. My wife, one of the kindest people you will ever meet, admits to me now that she lacked the courage to confront me for years. She needed something to spur her on.

One morning my friend James tugged his new dog Ben along to our house and asked me and Mojo to join them for a walk. It was the first meeting of these two very different dogs. Mojo was startled at first. She jumped about three inches in the air, yipped, and lunged straight for him. Now Ben was a Bernese mountain dog, a good-natured breed, placid with a side order of docile and a head the size of a shih tzu's body. He was an imposing figure, mostly black with some rust, a white horseshoe about the nose, and a white Swiss cross on his chest.

"He's a working dog," said James, possibly comparing him to mine.

"What kind of work does he do?" I responded.

My wife arrived about then, thinking what I was thinking. *One of these dogs is predator, the other prey.* But no director would ever put a tiny dog in the role of predator. Mojo bared her sharp little fangs and barked wildly. Ben's already low bushy tail fell even lower. He drew back. Great drops of sweat fell from the jowls of his ample mouth, which is the Bernese way of dealing with stress, I'm told.

It was no way to begin a friendship, but moments later all was forgiven as they walked side by side in some mutual agreement to at least leave one another alone. Ben loped happily along. Mojo pedaled as fast as she could to keep up. I noticed that our small dog remained between me and the Bernese. I have seldom admired this little dog more. Her bravery showed the lengths she would go to protect her master from a looming but gentle monster.

And so it was—perhaps by coincidence, perhaps not—that a few days later, my wife lunged at me.

I live in a world of words. I am constantly reading, writing, and speaking publicly. From early childhood I lay in bed tossing words in the air, seeing how they would land. Not Ramona. Every day in most conversations she struggles for the right words. It's frustrating for her. Years of epilepsy have not helped, but as the youngest of seven, her role was silence, and when she said, "Pass the salt," she said it eleven times to be heard.

When our psychologist friend Kevin Leman dragged Ramona and me onto a stage to ask questions about our marriage, she froze, horrified. I thought she did fine, but if she never sees another stage again, it will be too soon. I, on the other hand, was in my element. With Kevin talking about birth order, I confessed that we were both the youngest in our families.

"The babies have trouble making decisions," he said. "Is that you, Callaway?"

"Years ago I was indecisive," I smiled, "but now I'm not so sure."

As you might guess, I sometimes speak too much at home. In fact, when it comes to my words, the supply often exceeds the demand, and by the end of a conversation, I've usually said more than I meant.

A few days after the doggy introductions, Ramona and I argued. It doesn't matter what brought it about or who was right. What matters is that I said too much—again. My wife stood in the kitchen, leaning against the fridge, a dish towel in one hand, looking as if she'd like to strangle me with it. I had just presented my case, brilliantly arguing the merits of my point of view, my behavior, my rightness. She was silent. I waited. And then she lunged, punching me directly on the shoulder. This was not the sort of gentle love tap she had landed before. It was a direct hit containing all the force of the words she wished she could use. Worse, it was entirely warranted.

To my credit, I was speechless.

"You can argue circles around me." Ramona was fighting tears. "You can argue your way out of anything. I can't...I don't care if you're right...I just...your words hurt." And here she did the unthinkable. She began to cry.

If that isn't a turning point in a guy's marriage, he's an idiot. I hung my head. I opened my arms, moved toward her and said, "I'm sorry."

"Don't touch me," she said. "Don't...think of it. Back up. Just leave me alone. We'll talk later."

I opted for another walk with the dog. I told Mojo some things about what I was learning. "I've got some work to do," I said. And for one of the first times that day, I was right.

Change was coming because a little dog showed my wife how to stand up and sock me. "Thanks a lot," I said.

24

Everything Can Be Cleaned Up
Even Your Life

With a new dog—especially a small dog—it's important that you select the right food. I erred in this department at the start, and the result was a lot of nose plugging and mess cleaning. The Mojo of my youth could eat anything, but Mojo II had a delicate digestive tract. Dog food with corn in the ingredients did not linger long in her system, if you catch my drift. We tried just about everything and discovered to my horror that she responded well to the most expensive pet food in the history of the stuff. It is apparently handmade by Richard Branson.

Bad diet and easy potty training seldom coexist, but we discovered that covering the bathroom floor in newspaper and slowly taking a little newspaper away worked. The trouble was, she sometimes reverted to old habits and viewed that day's newspaper as a target. Which was okay, I suppose. Often the first few pages weren't worth reading anyway. The best material is in the classifieds, cartoons, and sports pages.

One day my brave new wife, emboldened by my brave new dog, dropped a subtle hint that I had been trying harder to understand my dog than I had my wife. I was heading off to speak at a conference at the time, and since Dr. Gary Chapman was there too, I decided to see what advice he could offer. Now Gary pretty much wrote the book on love—*The Five Love Languages*, which has inspired a hit song, been translated into forty-nine languages, and sold seven million copies in English alone. I was able to share a few meals with him, and as subtly as I knew how, I tapped this soft-spoken Southern gentleman for some marital wisdom.

We had met before at a conference in Hong Kong over a splendid three-hour version of Peking Duck. We reminisced about it, and then I asked, "Did you hear about the kid who was asked which language Santa speaks?" Gary hadn't. "North Polish," I said. Gary found this funnier than I thought he would.

"I have, um, a friend who's wondering which language his wife speaks," I said sneakily, as I'd done with Rick Warren, hoping Gary wouldn't notice that I was leaning forward.

"Well, the five love languages are these," he said, counting on one hand. "Words of affirmation—using words to affirm your spouse; acts of service—doing something for your spouse, like washing dishes, taking out the trash...anything you know they would like; gifts—they don't have to be expensive; quality time—giving them your undivided attention; and lastly, physical touch—holding hands, hugging, and the whole sexual part of the marriage."

"But how would this friend discover his wife's love language?"

Gary took a minute to answer as he was polishing off an assortment of veggies.

"Ask three questions. How does she express love to others? What does she complain about most often? What does she request most often? Her complaints might irritate you, but they give you valuable information. If she says, 'We don't ever spend time together,' you know her love language is quality time."

"Her complaints give me—I mean, this friend—her love language?"

"Absolutely." Gary was smirking. "If they're saying, 'Honey, can we take a walk after dinner tonight?' they're asking you for quality time. If they say, 'Would you give me a back rub?' it's physical touch. When you leave on a trip and they say, 'Be sure and bring me a surprise,' they're telling you that gifts are important to them."

"Okay. It's me. I'm the friend. But sometimes I don't get my wife." I'm sure it was the first time he'd heard of such a thing.

"We naturally speak our own language," said Gary, crunching a carrot. "So if words make me feel loved, I'll tell my wife how good-looking she is and how much I love her. But if her love language is acts of service and I'm not doing anything to help her, it's just a matter of time before she says, 'You keep saying you love me. Why don't you ever volunteer to help me?' I think I'm loving her, but she's not getting it."

"What is your wife's love language?"

Gary didn't have to think about this. "Acts of service. That's why I vacuum the floors or load the dishwasher. Karolyn is a happy woman, and she tells me I'm the greatest husband in the world. I value words of affirmation, so I feel loved. But it took me a long time to learn all that."

"My marriage hasn't been so…uh, smooth sailing lately. Was your marriage always good?"

Gary chuckled. And looked around for more veggies. "Six months after our wedding we were miserable. I was in seminary studying to be a pastor, but I just couldn't see how I could be this miserable and preach hope to people. Finally one night I said to God, 'I've done everything I can, and it's not getting any better.' As soon as I said that, there came to my mind a visual image of Jesus washing his followers' feet. And I heard God say, 'That's the problem in your marriage. You don't have the attitude of Christ.' It hit me like a ton of bricks. With all my Greek and Hebrew and theology, I had missed the whole point. I asked God to forgive me and give me the attitude of Christ toward my wife."

"I think my wife may be all five," I said. "No. But she loves serving others—I need to serve her. And words…words of affirmation."

"Ask her three questions. What can I do to help you? How can I make your life easier? How can I be a better husband? When you let her teach you how to serve her, her attitude toward you will change and she'll be asking you those questions."

The carrots were gone. The celery too. I think Gary was eyeing my plate. "No one gets married hoping to be miserable. They want a happy marriage."

"But may I confess something? I hate doing dishes."

This didn't surprise Gary either. "One man said to me, 'I understand the concept, and my wife tells me that her language is acts of service. But I'll tell you right now, if it's going to take my washing dishes and vacuuming floors for her to feel loved, you can forget that.' We're human. We have the power of choice. You can choose to love or not to love. If you feel loved by your spouse, the world looks pretty bright. For Karolyn and me, doing things God's way was really the turning point."

I thought about this for a few moments.

"Do the dishes," he said.

"May I take your plate?" I asked.

"You're gonna do fine," Gary smiled.

25

Sometimes It's Nice to Be Patted

Just before dark our dog went missing. I did a fast circle of the yard and then tapped on our suite door to recruit my dad. Mojo was sitting on his lap, eyes closed, leaning toward Dad, who was happily stroking her fur and patting her head. The two were becoming friends. Relieved, I smiled. "Sometimes it's nice to be patted," I said.

When I mentioned my comment to Ramona, she told me about a conversation she'd had at our aquatic center. Thinking she was alone, a lady in the change room was singing her heart out when Ramona came in. "Sing it, sister!" said my wife.

Instead of laughing, the gal said, "I'm sorry. I didn't know anyone was here. I'm so embarrassed."

"You sing beautifully," Ramona assured her. "You should sing more often."

Surprised by this, the lady replied, "Sometimes my mother told me not to sing. She never liked my voice."

"I like it," said my wife, "and I've got good taste in music."

Sometimes it's nice to be patted.

Thanks to Gary I decided that our home would be a place where words were used to build each other up. I asked some social media friends to help me by answering the question, "What is the nicest thing someone has ever said to you?"

Alfie wrote, "A nurse told me—after she flushed my ears—that I had the nicest ear canals she had ever seen."

Ed recalled the day a friend told him, "You look a lot like Clark

Gable." "I was flattered," said Ed, "until I considered the fact that Clark had been dead for 25 years."

Most of the answers were short and sweet. "I love you." "You're funny." "I forgive you." "Thank you." "I'm proud of you." "You changed my life." "You're a breath of fresh air." And the simple word "yes."

Shirley still recalls words someone spoke to her a decade ago. "You radiate God's love through your kindness and faith."

Sometimes it's nice to be patted.

Encouragement isn't always a good idea. One morning a man opened the door to get the newspaper and saw a strange little dog with the guy's newspaper in his mouth. He laughed and fed the dog some treats. The next morning the same dog was sitting there, wagging his tail, surrounded by eight newspapers.

"I will never forget the kind words a stranger spoke to me years ago on a Greyhound bus," wrote Shawn. "It had been a bad day. My husband was working out of town for more than a month. I was traveling with our two active children, aged two and three, when my eyeglasses snapped in half! I couldn't see a thing unless it was very close to me. So I read the kids story after story, trying to be quiet because some were sleeping around us. Suddenly my three-year-old interrupted, informing me that he had to go to the bathroom. I had just watched a man disappear into that bathroom, and he had not come out. So with my son bouncing up and down, I sang a song about a teddy bear to soothe him. When we finally reached our destination, I felt disheveled and exhausted. I sensed that everyone was glaring at me and my children. But as we exited the bus, a kind older lady looked me in the eye and said, 'You are such a wonderful mother.' Those words didn't just make my day, I've never forgotten them. Now I like to encourage other moms who may be having a particularly bad day too."

Solomon once wrote, "Some people make cutting remarks, but the words of the wise bring healing."[1] Words are like salt. When sprinkled rightly they can add flavor, melt ice, and preserve life. When misused they can sicken, sting, and corrode.

A few years ago I wrote about a frustrated high school teacher who told me, "You'll never amount to anything." Admittedly, I was not an easy addition to any classroom. But beneath my bold exterior, the words devastated me. Later that year, my English teacher, Mr. Bienert, said, "You have a gift. I want you in my communication arts class tomorrow morning."

I'm not overstating the fact—his words saved my life.

After publishing that story, I was startled by the response. Notes arrived from others who had heard those exact words the first teacher blurted out. Or this from a father: "Why can't you be like your brother?" Or this from a husband: "Why can't you keep this place clean?"

One came to see me. His name was Len. "I haven't amounted to anything," he said, sitting in my office. "It's like I've spent my life trying to prove the guy right."

"You're wrong," I said gently. I told him about my dog. How my son sometimes comes home with his shoulders slouched and his head down. But Mojo doesn't care about what others think of my son. Or his marks. Or his volleyball score. She just loves him. She meets him at the door with her tongue ready. She runs in circles, licking his face as if it were cheese, leaping in the air as if he were the last hope on the planet. No one is better at unconditional slobbers.

I watched a smile spread across Len's face.

"You're a much-loved child of the living God," I said. "You had the courage to tell me this. And I think today will mark a turning point for you."

The smile was still there, but the look was far away. "I had a dog once," he said. "Maybe I should buy another."

It's not just nice to be patted—it's necessary, it's transformative. Proverbs 18:21 warns, "The tongue can bring death or life." Words are seeds we sow without knowing they will produce plants. It's up to us to decide whether to plant flowers or weeds.

I'm just starting down this road, but there's hope ahead. When my wife asked me, "What's the nicest thing someone has ever said to you?" I said something sappy but true. "Well, many years ago a girl stood at the altar, looked me in the eyes, and said, 'I do.' And she did. Thanks, babe."

26

My Master Has the Really Good Stuff

Each Wednesday night Mojo disappeared. We couldn't figure it out at first. She'd paw at the door, and when I cracked it open, she was gone into the darkness. I had no idea she could move so fast. It's like asking an old man for a picture of his grandchild. I pulled on a light jacket and slippers and set off to find her. "Here puppy, here puppy." My voice changed octaves after ten frustrating minutes of this, but finally I found her behind the Turners' garbage bags, sniffing and clawing and snarfing up last Friday's chicken bones, her tail down. Ah, now I remembered—the next day was garbage day. I was not happy cleaning up, keeping a low profile, and dropping the busted bag into a fresh one.

I was vigilant with her leash for the next few Wednesdays, but then the cycle repeated itself. Dog escape. Sherlock activity. Spirited scolding. Dodging windows. Vigorous cleanup.

My wife shook her head each time. "Filthy dog. Put her on the leash."

"I know, I know. She escaped."

Thursday mornings were worse. Once she knew the delight concealed in those bags, there was almost no stopping her. I think she planned her weeks around garbage day, like a child plans winter around Christmas. Perched on the back of the sofa, the pup watched as neighbors carried treasure chests of goo and filth from their homes and dropped them curbside. And when Thursday morning brought the garbage man, she mourned the passing of those delicious bags as surely as that child mourns the passing of Christmas. Many of those

Thursdays she spent moping about, sick to her stomach, unable to help eat my breakfast.

I had always been surprised when she engaged in doglike behavior. Perhaps I personified this dog, humanized her. "Hey! You can't sniff *that*!" But a dog is forever a dog, continually returning to the disgusting.

Here again, I saw myself in my dog. More often than I care to admit, I am surprised by my own foolishness in returning to things that never satisfy, that later disgust and even sicken me.

My wife was the one who discovered the garbage cure.

The evening before and the morning of, she offered the hound a sniff of a dried apricot. Then she opened the door. The dog quickly took care of business and then rushed back indoors, prancing wildly at the prospect of a treat she enjoyed above all others.

Mojo loves apricots. When I hear her whining in delight during a dream, I know she is rolling in fields of dead gophers smothered in apricots.

Apricots. No more sickness. No more shame. And no more Sherlock activity needed on my part.

I don't remember the month we discovered this, but I do remember the day. I know it was the nineteenth because we were reading Psalm 19 just before bed, and I know it was a Wednesday because I had just tried my wife's garbage cure with great success and a happy dog was at my feet. These are the words I read.

> The instructions of the LORD are perfect,
>   reviving the soul.
> The decrees of the LORD are trustworthy,
>   making wise the simple.
> The commandments of the LORD are right,
>   bringing joy to the heart.
> The commands of the LORD are clear,
>   giving insight for living...
> The laws of the LORD are true;
>   each one is fair.

They are more desirable than gold,
  even the finest gold.
They are sweeter than honey,
  even honey dripping from the comb.
They are a warning to your servant,
  a great reward for those who obey them.

I once believed that God loved me and had a horrible plan for my life. I viewed God as a frowning deity. I just knew that if I climbed on his bus, I would be headed for misery. But these promises indicate the direct opposite. A 180-degree difference. Who wouldn't desire what revitalizes, imparts wisdom, brings joy and insight, is trustworthy and sweet, and promises great reward?

Being a dad has helped me view God in a different light. A dad loves his kids. He takes delight in their joy. Owning a dog has helped me view God in a different light as well. I can see the bigger picture. I know what will satisfy her in the end.

I'm old enough to have learned a few transforming truths. Few are more profound than this: As we honor and seek God and his kingdom, garbage bags on the curb become increasingly unattractive. I have seen the sickness they cause, and I find myself saying no more frequently to temporary pleasures, not because I don't want pleasure—we were wired for it—but because I want *true* pleasure, which only our Master has waiting for us when we come home.

27

Bury the Right Things

ojo had long since stopped enjoying my newspaper. And I was finally able to enjoy it myself. Sometimes it caused me to smile, as it did when I read a story from Washington State. A Seattle police station received a call that sounded intriguing enough to cause several officers to respond quickly. When they reached the scene of the crime, a flustered dog owner filled them in on what she called "an assault on her Chihuahua." She alleged that a man in her apartment complex had spit on her dog from an upper balcony. It was her first encounter with the suspect; she hadn't had problems with him before.

Police reportedly attempted to contact the suspect at his apartment, but no one came to the door. The official police report noted that the Chihuahua "was not seriously hurt." A top pranking officer could not resist adding that the dog "declined to speak with officers."

Now, I am not for spitting on dogs, and I don't suspect I'd be too excited were I in her sneakers, but the story was to hold a lesson for me before the weekend was out.

On Friday night we left for a camping trip in the Rocky Mountains with friends who promised steaks and pancakes and a white-knuckle river ride. The decision was easy. Saturday night my friend Larry and I climbed aboard an ATV, revved the throttle, and took off, him holding on to the handlebars and me gripping whatever I could find on the back. It was a breathtaking ride, but not in the way we had hoped. Easing down a steep embankment close to our camper, Larry made a ghastly mistake. He squeezed the front brake, and we flipped the thing. By which I do not mean we sold it for a profit.

Now these four-wheeled monsters weigh three or four times what we humans do. When you land amid rocks and brush and see the huge machine thundering down on you, there is no time to gather the children around and say a proper goodbye. My wife heard the awful sound of grinding metal and came running from the camper. Thankfully the ATV only rolled over parts of us, but I lay on my back stunned, oozing blood. My son arrived. And a medic from Afghanistan who yelled, "Secure the area!"

My funny bone still worked. "From what?" I asked. "Wolves?"

I don't remember saying this, but apparently I did.

The doctor in the Rednecksville hospital kept shaking his head, telling me I had no business surviving, that my family should be planning a funeral, and that the back of my head looked kind of like a cantaloupe. Apparently he took Bedside Manners 101 by correspondence.

"Wear a helmet next time," he said. And he was right.

I'll spare you the organ recital and just say that everything hurt. My rib cage was so badly torn that a sneeze felt like giving birth.

Along about Wednesday, the buzzing sound finally left, and I was grateful to be alive. But when I began reflecting on Larry's driving skills, bitterness began to eat at me like rust on my first car. Mojo was lying at my feet when the phone rang. It was Larry. He had one question on his mind. Would I forgive him? *Of course not,* I thought. *I'll just be quiet. I'd like the poor guy to sweat a bit. After all, my left side doesn't work, and I won't be able to golf for months.*

I was holding on to anger. And quite liking it. Oh sure, anger brings insomnia. And sore toes from kicking immovable objects. But to roll around in the possibility of vengeance gave me a measure of pleasure for a time.

Larry said it again. "I am so sorry. Can you forgive me?"

It may have been the pain medication, but these were the words that poured out. "Hey, I've done so many dumb things too, and people keep forgiving me. So yes. Absolutely. I forgive you."

Something shifted deep inside. Not my ribs, but something even deeper. It was like a load slid from my shoulders, and I found myself doing something I hadn't done in a week. Laughing. Which isn't funny when your ribs felt like mine.

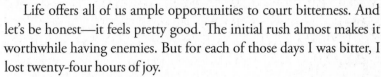

Life offers all of us ample opportunities to court bitterness. And let's be honest—it feels pretty good. The initial rush almost makes it worthwhile having enemies. But for each of those days I was bitter, I lost twenty-four hours of joy.

The only real cure for bitterness I've found is in the Bible: "Get rid of all bitterness, rage, anger, harsh words, and slander…Instead, be kind to each other, tenderhearted, forgiving one another, just as God through Christ has forgiven you."[1]

When I give in to bitterness, I become the very thing I disdain. Bitterness claps me in irons, cements my frown, and contradicts the behavior God showed me. When bitterness creeps up on me, I'm reminded that I follow a man whose first words amid blood, horror, and his hands nailed to a cross of wood were "Father, forgive." To the degree we remember what Jesus has done for us—to that degree we can forgive.

I have had to forgive myself too. For falling off a stage before a live audience. For forgetting a punch line on national television. For dropping barbells on my nose back in ninth grade (I'd rather not talk about it). Often we can't forget, but we can always forgive. It can be the start of a new way to remember. It can change the memories of past failures into hope for the future and free us up to laugh again.

I'm not eager to climb onto another ATV anytime soon, but when I do, I'll likely go with my friend Larry. I think he'll be more careful next time.

And I'll remember to take a cue from that hound in Seattle and the one at my feet. Don't get so worked up over things. Shake it off. Let it go. Bury it and walk away. Life can be good when you forgive and get on with living. Grudges are too heavy to ever pick up.

28

Wag More, Bark Less

We bought a Mojo-sized bed one day, padded with Styrofoam and covered in tan cloth. Thinking she'd thank us for it, I laid it out on the floor that night. "Come," I beckoned. She slinked past and then hopped onto our bed, which is akin to me hopping over a twenty-foot tree. Why do dogs do these things? Biologists say my dog loves my bed because it smells like me. My bed is where I sleep. And if you ask my wife, it's sometimes where I eat. Like me, canines prefer to sleep where it is temperate, where they can stretch out in safety, and where members of the family are close by. What's not to like about companionship and crumbs?

Harvard researchers, hoping to unearth secrets to a happy and purposeful life, studied 268 male Harvard undergrads from the classes of 1938–1940 (now well into their nineties) for 75 years. Unfortunately, the Harvard Grant Study didn't include women, but still it provides an unrivaled glimpse at what we value as time passes and what is most likely to make us happy and fulfilled.[1]

Their most significant finding was this: *Love is all we need.* George Vaillant, the psychiatrist who directed the study, claims that a man can have a successful career, plenty of money, and good physical health, but without supportive, loving relationships, he won't be happy. "Love is key to a happy and fulfilling life," says Vaillant. "The more areas in your life you can make connection, the better." The study found that strong relationships are by far the strongest predictor of a long and satisfying life.

Is it any wonder that more households have a dog than any other pet?[2]

When we asked three hundred dog lovers, "What do you enjoy most about owning a dog?" 56 percent said "companionship"—by far the most common word chosen. Of course we've all met dogs you wouldn't want to share a meal with, much less a bed, but for the most part it is impossible to contemplate a dog's gentle invasion of your home without asking, what can I learn about friendship from this dog? Here are some practical ideas.

Be the last to bark. The son of a minister saw his father's sermon notes, read them through, and noticed that his dad had penciled this remark in the margin: "Shout here, argument weak." Dogs don't say obvious things, like "If you really loved me you'd give me milk bones that taste like squirrels." They are compassionate living examples that less is truly more when it comes to words. There's a time to state your case and draw your lines, but even when you are right, be the last to yell.

Make up fast. My dog has taught my wife and me to never let the sun go down on our wrath. So we stay up and fight. It's the same with relationships outside marriage. When I came running around a corner and accidentally kicked my dog, it was startling how quickly my apology was met with jumping and pouncing. Let things go faster.

We were made to carry more on our shoulders than a chip.

Lick wounds. Her father died when she was eight, family life was difficult, and her spiritual life was at times painful, yet Mother Teresa was loved the world over because she showed up to carry burdens and offer comfort. Like the dog, we were made for this. When we roll up our sleeves and get involved helping the hurting, we discover that we'll never be short of friends.

Having spoken through the years at men's events, I can tell you that we guys converse fluently on matters that don't matter at all. But ask us who we would go to if we were about to have an affair, were tempted to rob our employer, or learned we had cancer, and many of us don't have a clue. Finding friends was a piece of cake for me in high school. Then I went to college. Got married. Got in-laws. Mortgages, kids, a lawn mower…pretty soon, friends were guys I hadn't seen in twenty years. Maybe that's why a dog became so appealing to me.

A dog offers us the gift of simply being there. In the good times.

And bad. We can cry with a dog present. And be a bit of a fool. A dog brings to a friendship sincerity, enthusiasm, interest, dedication, passion, and a fair amount of drool. A dog reminds us that the intentional cultivation of deep, meaningful friendships can increase our effectiveness, our happiness, and even our life expectancy.

A dog taught me to be the kind of friend I'd like to have as a friend.

29

I Only Have Eyes for You

They say that people who stay married can live four years longer than those who don't.[1] I mentioned this to someone and he frowned. "Yeah, well, that's just four more years of misery," he said.

"That's really up to you," I replied. "I love being married."

"How many years you been married?" he asked.

"Thirty-two."

"In a row?"

"Yep."

"Four different women?"

"Nope. Just one."

"How?"

"Small miracles along the way," I said. "Plus I stopped saying dumb things like, 'If it makes you feel better, I'll pretend I'm wrong.'"

"Anything else?"

"My dog helped. A dog doesn't say dumb things, like 'If it will make you feel better, I'll pretend you're right.'"

He almost choked. "You said that?"

"Yep." Then I told him three or four more tricks my dog taught me that helped save my marriage. He didn't take notes, but he listened.

Before this little hound arrived, our unresolved arguments followed a disturbing pattern. My opening barrage was almost always accusatory and negative. "How could you buy towels? We have three towels already!"

"But they were on sale. And the old towels are...old."

"Well, that's an old excuse," I said, which was an attempt at sarcasm and made no sense at all.

"If you hadn't bought that golf club," she countered, "maybe we could afford towels."

Complaint was getting me nowhere, so I turned to criticism and comparison. "Why don't you save us some money by making towels? I think my mother made all our towels when I was a kid."

"Well, maybe you should ask your mother to make some for us. And some soup. You keep telling me her soup is amazing."

"Maybe I will."

In time I began to notice that complaint and criticism had turned to a deadly killer called contempt. And I knew it was the one thing our marriage couldn't survive. Fueled by negative thoughts about my wife, I began to blame her. Then disengage, shut down, and distance myself by turning away. I was steering toward disaster.

And how did a dog help change all this? By showing me four subtle tricks.

I will pay attention. It happened when Ramona was doling out peanut butter, of course, but the dog's attention went far deeper than that. Mojo followed her around the house. When my wife moved from the kitchen to the bedroom, you could hear the click-clack of her toenails (the dog's) on the hardwood, and for me something clicked into place.

When I got home at night, I resolved that instead of turning on the TV or computer, I would humble myself, enter the kitchen, and actually converse with my wife. I would not talk about towels; I would just see how she was doing. I opened with "What's up, Doc?" In the early years of our marriage, reading books and magazine articles together was a favorite activity, but it had vanished with our hectic lifestyle. I would resurrect it. While she made dinner, I sat on a stool, pulled on my reading glasses, and read out loud.

"Why are you reading to the dog?" she asked at first.

"I'm not," I said. "I'm reading to you."

I decided to give it a month and see what happened. On day one her countenance had already changed. "Thanks," she said on day two. "I love this."

I will be quick to show affection. Those who encounter me and my dog while we're walking don't stand and analyze her. They stoop and touch her. And with the exception of wiggly toddlers, she eagerly returns their affection.

"Affection," said the dog lover C.S. Lewis, "is responsible for nine-tenths of whatever solid and durable happiness there is in our lives." Showing my wife affection, not just with touch but also with words, changed our marriage. And it was easier than I thought it would be. "Know what I appreciate about you?" I said. Then I just filled in the blanks. Another time, just for fun, I hopped up beside her, put my chin on her knee, looked adoringly upward, and breathed a deep sigh of content. "Who am I?" I asked.

"Down, boy," she said.

I will stop critiquing the housework. I had allowed subtle negative thoughts to poison my attitude toward Ramona and all she did. Increasingly she could do nothing right. One day she said, "I walk on eggshells around you." And I knew she was right.

The change came first from some healthy self-talk. I reminded myself of what I loved about her from the start. I recalled admirable qualities, reflected on how gorgeous she was, and began focusing on what she did well. This led to the realization of how valuable she was.

One day I genuinely complimented her on some beef veggie soup. I'm sure there were times she had thought of poisoning my broth, but this soup was to die for.

Without a hint of sarcasm, I added, "My mother never came close to making soup this good." She seemed shocked. Speechless. Finally, she grinned and stuck her tongue out at me. I wish I would have had a camera.

I will only have eyes for you. No other animal makes and maintains eye contact with us—particularly when we're eating—like the dog. Dogs look into our eyes. They return our gaze. Try this with a chimpanzee at the zoo, and he will launch into a fit, chattering and prancing from limb to limb, viewing your gaze as aggression. But dogs look us in the eye, an essential key to healthy communication in any relationship.

I once thought that the secret to sparking romance with my wife was a candlelit dinner that cost too much or a weekend getaway. Mojo showed me another way and saved me a bundle of money too—look into her eyes. Turn toward her rather than away. Romance grows in the daily grind when a couple is driving along in silence and he says, "Look! A Ford Pinto! Remember?" And she smiles and says, "No. But remind me." Turning toward each other rather than away can keep you happily married for sixty years.

While Ramona was shopping one day, I stopped by a car lot just for fun. A salesman latched on to me, stroked a late model Toyota, and enticed me with a zero-percent interest payment plan I'd be a fool not to take advantage of.

"Man," I laughed, "I don't buy pants without my wife's advice. I won't be buying a car."

He gave me a look that would wilt a sturdy oak. "You're kidding. You let your wife tell you about cars?"

"Yep," I said. "Don't you?"

"No."

"How's that working?" I asked.

"Well, um…" he stammered, "we're divorced."

Years ago we agreed during one of those everyday turn-toward-each-other moments that we wouldn't spend more than a hundred bucks without allowing the other to influence the decision. I don't think it saved our marriage, but it didn't hurt. Such tricks help nurture an affection that overlooks our faults and failures.

The disagreements did not end. But they became more and more tolerable. A little like tickling, I suppose. That gentle attack from someone you trust enough to know they really won't hurt you.

I suppose the best marriages happen when we pay attention and covet familiarity with each other's world. In time my fondness and admiration grew. I came to know what thrilled, worried, irritated, and stressed her. I could tell you her favorite dessert, getaway, movie, and childhood memory. I even learned her shoe size, her best friends' names, and what she most liked to shop for. Towels weren't even on the list.

30

Don't Jump from the Train
When You're in a Tunnel

Perhaps the reason dogs find us so wonderful is that they are blessed with startlingly low expectations. My wife learned this trick from the dog, and I am grateful each and every day. She was absolutely ecstatic once when I unclogged a sink. I merely ran some water, yelled down the hole, and it unplugged. I'm not sure why, but it worked fine from then on. Another time I oiled a squeaky door for her. She was so impressed, she almost wept. Low expectations are a great gift we can bring to any relationship.

We still didn't see eye to eye on everything of course. When couples do, one of them likely isn't necessary. Sadly, my wife learned something else from our dog. Though some dogs seem eager to stockpile, they are rare. You just don't find a dog pulling his toys down the street in a wagon. Ramona learned to get rid of stuff. To just heave them out. Once I caught her sneaking two bags of my personal belongings into the trunk destined for the thrift store. Perfectly good stuff. Cassette tapes. A beautiful watch that didn't tick but had golf club hands. Pants that fit me nicely (when I was in high school).

"Hey," I said. "At this rate we'll never be on that hoarder's TV show." And I was right.

Now this is all good and well, but some things shouldn't be tossed out.

A reporter asked a couple how they had managed to stay married sixty-five years. The husband didn't seem to hear the question, but his wife did. She replied, "We were born in a time when if something was broken, we would fix it, not throw it away." They both knew one of the great secrets to the good life: Don't jump from the train when you're in a tunnel. They followed through on what they knew to be right and had the humility to work on things when all the world said, "Chuck it and run."

I grew up in the 1960s, which was the golden age of fixing stuff. Living below the poverty line, we didn't pitch anything. Except a baseball that had no cover. We kept stuff. If it was broken, we fixed it.

Mom reused aluminum foil and tea bags sometimes. She could get thirteen pots of tea from one tea bag. Then she made soup with it. And salad. Then we flossed with the string. Once she helped me tape and nail together a broken baseball bat—it was one of the few things that didn't take. She waxed floors so they would last longer. She hemmed pants for me. My brother's pants. They lasted years. Mom even made her own birthday cards.

Dad never dreamed of anyone else changing the oil in our car or of buying shoes when he could hobble over to Henry's Shoe Repair shop. He showed me how to repair bicycle inner tubes, what a carburetor did, and where to buy string and glue.

I thought everyone was as poor as we were, which would have made everyone astoundingly rich. You see, we had a dog. A garden. Hand-me-down bicycles. And a pond for catching frogs. We grew our own food, crafted our own Christmas ornaments, made our own Christmas candles, and sold them door-to-door. We even made our own tie-dyed shirts. We were so cool that summer we didn't even need air-conditioning.

Throwing things out would have meant there was more where that came from, and there simply wasn't. We lived that close to the edge. I suppose growing up in an age of fixing up showed me that you can refurbish more than radios and lawn mowers and fridges and children's toys. You can fix friendships. You can mend a marriage.

All this talk of the last century can make us a little nostalgic, and it's important to remember that the good old days weren't all good. If you need proof, visit an outhouse, do without electricity for a year, and store ice cream in a dank cellar surrounded by ice blocks. The writer of Ecclesiastes warns us, "Don't long for 'the good old days.' This is not wise."[1]

But we can ask a very wise question that my dog seems to ask with regularity: How do I live right now? Micah 6:8 gives the answer: Do what is right, love mercy, and walk humbly with God. We can't do anything about 1963 or last Wednesday, but we can do something about today.

Certainly this includes binding up the broken, fixing friendships, and mending marriages. I guess I'll start by thanking Ramona for knowing what to throw out and what to hang on to. I'm glad she hung on to me. Even if she's about to throw out a tie-dyed shirt that was best before 1973.

31

Love Your Enemies
After All, You Made Them

If you've ever doubted whether dog is man's best friend, try an experiment. Lock your wife and your dog in the bathroom for about twenty minutes. When you open the door, see who's glad to see you.[1] Is there any more endearing attribute in a dog than its capacity to forgive and forget?

One evening amid all my busyness, I noticed Mojo sitting by her empty dog dish and staring at me, modeling two divine attributes—patience and hope. And when finally I loaded those pans to the brim, she modeled another virtue with a frantic wagging of her tail—forgiveness.

I love the story of some soldiers during the Korean War who hired a local kid to cook and clean for them. Unfortunately for the poor houseboy, these guys were pranksters. They loved playing jokes on him, and he was a bit naive. They'd smear Vaseline on the stove handles, and by the time he'd turned the stove on first thing in the morning, his fingers were slicker than, well, Vaseline on a stove. They put water buckets above the door so he'd get a cold shower when he swung the door open. Once they even nailed his shoes to the floor during the night. When he fell for the pranks, they laughed until they had to sit down.

The poor kid took it pretty well. Like my dog, he didn't say much. As a result, they started to like him. So much so that they finally felt guilty and sat the young Korean down. "Hey, we know these pranks aren't funny anymore. We're sorry. We won't take advantage of you again."

The houseboy's eyes grew wide. "No more sticky on stove?"

"Nope."

"No more water on door?"

"Nope."

"No more nail shoes to floor?"

"Nope, never again."

"Ah," said the boy. "Then I no more spit in soup."

Rarely do we find someone with the capacity to forgive without the need to spit in our soup. It may be my dog's forgetfulness or her small stature, but vengeance is not on her daily planner. I accidentally step on her tail in the kitchen and her ears fall backward and her tail plummets. As I reach for her and say, "Sorry!" she wags everything. This dog is positively eager to not wait one more moment to forgive.

As another year sped by, a longtime business relationship soured. Things agreed to by phone and never put in writing were denied by the other party. I had no recourse but to watch as my ideas were put to work and I lost a sizable income. Anger swelled within me like a sponge in water. At night I lay awake steaming and stewing and imagining conversations in which my brilliant comebacks made perfect sense, humiliated my foe, and mended bridges. But when my daylight attempts at reconciliation fell flat, I began to consider how a judge would see things.

Waking at four one morning, I paced the house. A dog has nothing scheduled during those hours, so Mojo walked a few paces behind, her claws click-clacking the hardwood. When I sat on the sofa, she hesitated and then hopped aboard. I told her everything. The resentment. The regret. The thoughts of revenge. As I heard myself talk, it became apparent that continuing on this path was a sure spiral downward. Like a bee that dies when it stings, a part of me was dying too. *Psychology Today* reports that there is one surefire way to be happier and live longer. It is to forgive.[2] But if you want to profit from the life-extending benefits of forgiveness, don't wait for others to apologize. Start the process within you.

Back in twelfth grade, a girl I loved more than anything on earth dumped me. The knot in my stomach made sleep impossible. In the middle of the night, I picked up a small Bible my mother had left by my bed and thumbed through it, hoping for words of comfort. Instead I read words I thought were impossible at the time: "Get rid of all bitterness, rage, anger."[3]

Come on, God, I thought. *I'm hurt. Rejected.* But for some reason I kept on reading: "Be kind to each other, tenderhearted, forgiving one another, just as God through Christ has forgiven you."[4] *But God,* I thought, *I'm humiliated. Hurt. Wondering what people are thinking of me. I can't face a future where everything has shifted.* One word kept coming back to me. It wasn't audible, but it was just as clear: Forgive.

You can't forgive without loving. You can't love without forgiving.

The Bible teaches that Jesus canceled my debt at Calvary, and I in turn must cancel the debts others have built up against me. It's far from easy, but it's essential. At first, forgiveness feels like I'm rewarding my enemy. But one good look at the cross where Jesus died, and forgiveness becomes a gift from one undeserving soul to another, a gift that frees me from the prison of my own anger and bitterness.

It didn't make a whole lot of sense to me until I experienced this forgiveness myself through my wife, my kids, my dog, and God himself. I began to focus not on what has been done *to* me, but what has been done *for* me. The first leads to bitterness. The second to thanksgiving.

"Thanks, God," I said out loud. "Thanks for your forgiveness. Help me spread it around."

Lifting the sleeping dog from my lap, I carried her to the bedroom and gently placed her on the floor. Then I climbed into bed beside my wife, that former girlfriend I had learned to forgive.

The Best Treats Are Those You Don't Deserve

A quick Internet search reveals hundreds of videos of dogs who have been taught by their masters to say grace. Some are howlingly funny. But a dog is even better at living grace than saying it. My dog seems to stand eagerly by, just waiting for a chance to extend this gift in the face of my forgetfulness or neglect through excessive travel. Grace. We can't breathe without it. And if we sit up and pay attention, a furry little creature's grace can teach us to be more gracious to others.

Sometimes we see the gift of grace in an international superstar, and it is unforgettable. On May 31, 1987, my son Stephen turned one, and Clint Eastwood blew out fifty-seven candles. In the wild world of sports, the Edmonton Oilers beat the Philadelphia Flyers to claim hockey's holy grail, the Stanley Cup.

Russell Shoeppe was there. And he will never forget that night.

Earlier in the day, Russell and a friend somehow secured press passes, and after the game they sneaked into the Oilers' locker room to celebrate with the team. They drank from the cup, patted players' backs, and then stole superstar Wayne Gretzky's helmet, stuffed it under a jacket, and left the building.

For many years that light blue helmet with the number ninety-nine adorned a shelf at Russell's business. "Trust me," said Russell, "it was the greatest conversation starter a guy could have." It was also a trophy of a life devoted to nobody but Russell.

After I spoke somewhere, he told me the helmet story with wide eyes and a tentative grin. "I saw a television interview with the Edmonton Oilers' equipment manager once," he added. "He was asked if people sometimes stole the players' equipment for souvenirs and memorabilia. He said no. He prided himself on guarding things vigilantly. 'People tried to steal Wayne Gretzky's equipment all the time, but I tricked them by putting Wayne's name on equipment bags. People stole them, but I stuffed those bags with towels.' Next he was asked if anyone ever managed to steal something from Wayne. He laughed and said, 'Well, there was this once…'"

"My life was coming off the rails, man. I was far from God." Russell's dark eyes flashed and then softened. "Then I met Jesus. I'm following him now. My wife just told me we're expecting our first. It's great. But it's scary. The doctor says it's a boy. I can't help thinking that I still have that helmet. How can I ever show it to my son? What will I say?

"I've got one more confession." He grinned. "I'm a golfer."

"There's forgiveness for that too," I said.

"Would you sign this?" Russell asked. He handed me a copy of a golf book I'd written. I smiled and took it from him and then wrote in the front, "For Russell. Give Wayne his helmet back."

Months passed. Then a year. I had forgotten about the helmet, of course, amid the stuff of life, the concerns of kids, caring for parents and a scruffy little dog.

One day an email arrived from Russell. He had written Wayne Gretzky and told him of his newfound faith and of a burden he had carried for many years. "I'm sorry for swiping your helmet," he told Wayne. "It was stupid. It was wrong. I'm a father now, and I want to do the right thing. Just tell me where to send the helmet."

Wayne had written back, saying he was deeply touched. "Keep the helmet on two conditions," he wrote. "Never sell it. And give it to your son when he is old enough to understand the story."

When summer arrived, Russell and I went golfing to celebrate. Wayne couldn't make it, but my son Jeffery came along. I wanted him to hear Russell's story because few things shape your child's life like seeing other lives changed. Here we were, listening to a story of grace while playing the most graceless game ever invented. In golf, if the wind moves your ball when you're ready to hit it, you count a stroke. You move a twig and your ball moves? Count a stroke. Your ball lands in a tree? Too bad. Climb the tree and hit it or take another stroke. No wonder some Scotsman invented the mulligan. To me, it is one of the most beautiful words in the English language.

Days earlier I had spent time talking with Philip Yancey about a book he had written on the topic of grace. Philip said something I hadn't forgotten, and I mentioned it to Russell. "I left the church for a time because I found such little grace there. I returned because I found it nowhere else." We talked about Wayne and the fact that there is no more endearing characteristic in a friendship or a marriage, in a church or a faith, as grace quickly offered.

I had just missed a three-foot putt. "Dog biscuits!" I said, which caused my son to laugh.

"I once asked a former Buddhist what he found in Jesus that he discovered nowhere else. He smiled and simply said, 'Forgiveness for my sins.'"

"So true," said Russell.

Wayne Gretzky was once asked why he scored almost twice as many points as anyone else in the history of hockey. He answered, "I skate to where the puck is going to be, not where it has been." We were on the eleventh hole when I told Russell this. He was beating me soundly by then, but it wasn't the score that made him smile. "I've made plenty of mistakes. I can't go back. But I can do the right thing today and move forward with God's help."

I hope Russell buys his son a dog to remind him every day of God's grace. But until he does, a light blue helmet with the number ninety-nine sitting atop his dresser should do the trick quite nicely. Soon the boy would be old enough to ask again and again for the story of how this trophy of God's grace got there. He would hear the story of how his dad met Wayne and got the helmet autographed. How a collector contacted his dad and offered him a nice sum of money. Twenty-five thousand bucks. And how his dad didn't even flinch. Like grace, some things are not for sale. They can only be passed along.[1]

33

The Best Things Are Difficult
Before They Become Easy

The years flew by. Marks on a tattered measuring chart taped to our pantry door bore proof—children grow up fast. Dogs too. The boys even changed their names. Stephen to Steve. Jeffery to Jeff. When they were small, we begged them to finish their broccoli. Now they finished their broccoli. And ours. They cleaned out the pantry too. Then the fridge. And the freezer. Everything but the dishwasher. When they were small we prayed they would stop screaming and sleep through the night. Now, on Saturday mornings, not even the dog could wake them up. Pouncing on them, she licked their eyes and ears without success. They groaned, rolled over, and slept like teenagers.

Most nights Mojo slept at Rachael's feet. And when the sun rose, the dog just sat there, waiting, hoping, modeling unreasonable patience.

Boys in our daughter's class took notice of her. So much so that shortly after she turned sixteen, she taped a Bible verse to her bedroom door—"Be merciful to me, O God, for men hotly pursue me."[1] And they did. Boy did they ever. Arriving home from work one day, I was informed by a nod of my wife's head that I'd better go to my daughter's room.

I tapped on the door. "Come in."

She sat on her bed squeezing the dog tightly and sniffling. Beside the two of them lay a dozen red roses.

"What's wrong?"

She just hugged the dog for a minute and then through tears told me of a visit from an upperclassman who asked if she would consider dating him. "I said no." More sniffling.

"How come?"

"He's not the kind of guy I wanna marry. Why would I date him?"

I gently asked why the tears. "He was a good friend. I guess that's gone. He can't be now." Mojo stretched upward and licked her face. Picking up the flowers, Rachael added, "I doubt the right one will ever come along."

"Ah, sweetie. You be patient. Like that dog."

"She's single, Dad."

Laughter helped at such times. Especially when I didn't instigate it.

"You want to know something I fail at more than just about anything else, Rachael? Patience. I admire patience in the driver behind me, but not the one in front."

She smiled and sniffled a happier sniffle.

"Last night I asked Mom to trim my neck hairs. She said she would but kept doing other stuff. 'What's taking so long?' I asked, and I wasn't very nice about it. She trimmed my neck hairs, and then she pinched me. Hard."

Rachael raised her eyebrows. "Where?"

"On the…seat of my understanding."

"What did you do?"

"Well, after she crawled into bed, I flipped the light off and said to her, 'When you're ready to apologize to me, I'll be right over here.'"

Rachael laughed. "Did Mom laugh?"

"Yes, she did. Her laugh has kept us married all these years."

"Ah, that's sweet."

I held her close. "You know something, Rachael? Whoever lands you will be the luckiest guy on the planet. You be patient. Keep praying. God loves you, and he listens."

"So does the dog," she sniffled. And then the tears were back.

Dinner that night was chicken worthy of a Martha Stewart cover, but when my son's friend Chris arrived, we knew we'd best find something to supplement it. Chris could eat like a horse but never settled for hay. Once I found him in our kitchen, sucking on a gallon of milk. The fact that I didn't yell at him helped forge our friendship. Mojo greeted Chris with tall leaps and much wagging. After dinner my sons left, but he stayed—just sat in the living room, the dog straddled atop his knees.

"How you doing?" I asked.

He couldn't talk at first, just sat there massaging the dog's shoulders, his head down. Finally Chris muttered, "Mojo. You're so…loyal." More silence.

"I'm sorry."

"Thanks. We'll get through it. It's just…hard."

A big football-loving kid, Chris stood more than six feet, and when he swung a golf club, his father and I would stand back and say, "Wow!" But the last year or so the golf games with his father stopped, and when his dad had an affair and walked out, he and his sisters were devastated. We talked often, and this simple comment about the dog summed up his disappointment with his dad.

When asked what a dog has taught them about life, 15 percent of our respondents mentioned either loyalty or faithfulness. This trait has endeared dogs to us through the centuries as surely as a faithful father endears himself to a watching son. But when loyalty is missing, our world can fall apart.

"You know something?" Chris said. "It would have hurt worse if it was you. I've always looked up to you. With Dad, well, I saw this coming for years."

I was stunned. "Oh man. I'm so prone to wander. That could just as easily have been me, Chris. All our lives we live just one decision away from disaster. Let's make sure you and I stay faithful and loyal just one moment at a time. All your life you'll have two voices whispering in your ear. Go with the softer voice. The louder one will still pop up, but not so often."

Rachael arrived then, carrying a dozen roses. *Maybe this tall long-ball golfer was the one she was praying for,* I thought.

She raised the flowers and handed them to Chris. "I want you to give these to your mom," she said. I have rarely been more proud.

I brought the dog into her room that night, plunked Mojo on her bed, and said goodnight. Rachael bent over and gave the pup a smooch. This is an exact transcript of our conversation.

"Rachael, don't kiss the dog."

"Why not?"

"Puppies lick your face because they like their mother to regurgitate food for them. Are you able and willing to do this?"

"Gross."

"You should save kissing for your husband."

"But I don't have a husband."

"You will one day. Then what will he think if he finds out you kissed the dog?"

"I won't tell him."

"He'll know."

"How?"

"Dog hair gets stuck to your lips and never leaves."

"Dad, I think Mom's calling you."

"Goodnight."

"Goodnight."

"Love you."

"Love you too. I'm kissing the dog."

And she was.

34

I've Got Today
Tomorrow Is None of My Beeswax

We celebrated Mojo's seventh birthday at Rachael's insistence. Since she was the lone one among us who remembered the date each year (June 6), we allowed her to rip the wrapping off the presents and present them to the dog: a chew toy and some treats that doubled as doggy toothbrushes.

The year had been one of celebration for us. Our son completed his first year of college, and Ramona was doing great. "How's your wife?" people often asked. I thanked them and said, "Hey, she's doing great. She has me."

It was our first formal birthday party for the hound. Gathered at the table, the kids began to recount memories of life with this dog. The first caused us all to cringe.

During the summer of Mojo's third year, Steve and Jeff had been playing baseball in a nearby field. One was pounding fly balls to the other when the dog, hoping to get in on the action, I suppose, was struck in the head by a sharply hit grounder. I was rounding the side of the house when I saw them running toward me. Steve was carrying the dog. Both boys were pale and unable to speak. "She's...she's..." He couldn't bring himself to say the word "dead."

The dog's eyes were open but unseeing. Her tongue was hanging limply from her mouth. "It's okay, you guys," I said. "It's okay."

Taking Mojo gently from him, I stroked her head. I could feel something like a faint heartbeat, so we jumped in the car together and took off.

By the time we arrived at the veterinarian's clinic, the dog was starting to stir. And when the vet administered a shot of some sort, she assured me, "The dog will be fine. No playing baseball for a while though."

Our moods were better as we left. I even pointed and smiled at the sign on the vet's door: "Back in five minutes. Sit. Stay."

"What has the dog taught you about life?" I asked.

"To be careful with baseballs," said Jeff, who was stuffing dentist-approved treats down Mojo's gullet.

"To just be nicer to people," said Rachael. "You never have to wonder if a dog really likes you."

"You mean we should wag the right thing?" I asked.

Rachael raised her eyebrows and rolled her eyes. We all knew why. She hadn't been receiving flowers from all of her friends lately. One long-time BFF had turned on her, gossiping fluently to the other girls at school. Forgiveness was slow in coming, but the dog was teaching her some things too.

"Maybe a dog has so many friends because he wags his tail, not his tongue."

They liked that idea.

"It's no coincidence that man's best friend can't say anything," said Steve. College had made the boy even smarter.

"When Mojo hangs out with Chewie, she has no brains at all," said Jeff, speaking of the incorrigible little relative of Mojo's next door.

"Ah, friends," said Ramona. "You feel better and act better when you're with good friends. You behave better."

It was like my dog was preaching to my kids. But I couldn't resist adding, "Be like Mojo. Choose your humans wisely."

"Sit up," said Jeff, enticing the dog with another treat.

"Exactly," I said. "Sit up and pay attention to life. Brilliant, Jeff."

"Huh?"

"I think you guys are in danger of being a generation of watchers. Of missing what is engaging and stretching because you're staring at your phones."

"Amen," said Ramona.

"Did I ever show you the cartoon of the guy and girl sitting in a restaurant? He's staring at his phone. She says, 'If I tape your phone to my forehead, will you find me interesting?'"

"Yes, Dad," said Rachael. "Ten times."

"I just don't want to end up like some of the families we see who don't talk in restaurants. They stare at gizmos. The kids text Mom what they want for supper so she can email Dad and he can fax the waiter."

"You don't have to worry," said Jeff as he pulled the last treat from the bag. "We know the restaurant rule."

Though we'd only done it once, they knew that each was to put his or her phone in the middle of the table. The first to pick it up also picked up the check.

"A dog doesn't worry," said my wife, and we all knew why she said it.

Her brother Dennis had finally succumbed to Huntington's after being curled up in the fetal position for ten years in a long-term care facility. Her sisters Miriam and Cynthia were in nursing homes now, their bodies and minds slowly failing them. Their husbands, Jim and Bill, were doing all they could, but the future was clouded with uncertainty. Each time the phone rang, Ramona wondered.

"Don't worry, Mom," said Rachael. "It'll be okay."

It was a great time to ask a favor, so I did. "Would you kids do dishes? Mom and I want to go for a walk."

"Just leave your cell phones here," said Steve. "You two need to communicate."

"You know the best way to keep your kids out of hot water?" I said, as I shut the door. "Put dishes in it."

She held my hand as we took the dog on a leisurely stroll. Upon our return I decided to wage war on some dandelions. Ramona transplanted some flowers. And uncollared Mojo eyed us from the front deck.

Suddenly, she spied a cat across the street and took off after it as if she'd been shot out of a gun. I could hear a van coming down the street. Fast. "Stop," I yelled. But there was nothing I could do. It was too late. We watched in horror as Mojo skidded beneath the van. She entered just behind the front tire and shot out the back. "Please, no." The dog let out a timid "Yip," picked herself up, sat down, cocked her head, and looked at me. She just sat, dazed and blinking, this dog with nine lives. I had always doubted that dogs have guardian angels. That night I wasn't so sure.

Ramona saw the whole thing and stood there, holding some petunias, stunned. I picked up the pup and carried her over to Ramona. "You know what? God cares about a little dog," I said. "I've got to believe he'll take care of your family too."

35

It's Difficult to OD
on Optimism

A week after my friend James adopted his new dog Max, he brought the Lab by for a test drive. We were enduring the coldest winter in thirty years, and the previous day's snowstorm had piled drifts so high you could barely see the top of an eight-foot cedar in our front yard. I had been grousing about the weather, but Max didn't seem to mind. He plunged through the snow, biting chunks off, leaping in the air like he had a new leash on life.

And he did. Details of the first six months of his life were sketchy, and there were classic signs that it had not gone well until James and Anne brought him to a caring home.

"At what age is it appropriate to tell your dog he was adopted?" I asked as I collared Mojo.

James shook his head at my humor and looked at me like I was beyond help.

"Come on, that was funny," I said. "Did I tell you Mojo is starting to go deaf?"

"No. Sorry about that."

"I was thinking about this. If my dog goes blind, can I get a Seeing Eye dog for my dog?"

James shook his head again, and the four of us set off, scrunching through the snow in the bright afternoon sun.

"So why is it that any altercation between a small dog and a big dog leaves the large dog at fault—even if the big dog is tied up in your backyard?" muttered James.

"Did something happen this week?"

James nodded his head vigorously. "This dog is driving us nuts," he confided. "Our cat Percy is going out of her mind."

"What does he do?"

"Chases her. Eats her cat food. Nips at her tail."

Until this brash, confident, overly vivacious dog arrived, the cat ruled the house.

"Percy just sits there and glares at Max, wishing he'd go away."

James had removed Max's leash, and off the dog went, diving into drifts and then turning to look at us with a snort, his face coated in white.

Mojo was twelve now. She trotted along beside us, high-stepping and happy but lacking the body to plunge into these insurmountable drifts like the wound-up newcomer. Nothing went unnoticed in Max's world. Everything excited him. If he could speak, he might say, "A walk in the snow! Incredible! No leash for six minutes! Amazing! A car ride and a tummy rub on the same day! Are you kidding me? My humans will have table scraps later! How can you beat that? Then I'll visit the neighbor's garbage can! It's the best! Then maybe watch TV with my people! Can it get any better? Sleeping on their bed! Yes! It can get better!"

Once we were home and the coffee was on, we joked about Max's youthful exuberance. Someone had sent me a cat's diary, penned by Anonymous, so I rooted around until I found it. James laughed as I hit on the highlights. It sounded like poor Percy.

> Day 983 of my captivity:
>
> My captors continue to taunt me with bizarre little dangling objects.
>
> They dine lavishly on fresh meat, while I am fed some sort of dry nuggets. I make my contempt for the rations perfectly clear, but must eat something in order to keep up my strength. What keeps me going is my dream of escape.
>
> In an attempt to disgust them, I once again brought up my lunch on the carpet. Then I decapitated a mouse and

dropped its headless body at their feet. I thought this would strike fear into their hearts, since it clearly demonstrates what I am capable of. However, they merely made condescending comments about what a "good little hunter" I am. They are insane.

I was placed in solitary confinement when some of their accomplices arrived for dinner. I could hear the noises. I could smell the food. I overheard that my confinement was due to the power of "allergies." I must learn what this means and how to use it to my advantage.

Today I was almost successful in an attempt to assassinate one of my tormentors by weaving around his feet as he was walking. I must try this again tomorrow at the top of the stairs.

The dog is a flunky and a snitch. He is regularly released and seems more than willing to return. He obviously belongs to a slower group.

The bird must be an informant. My captors have arranged protective custody for him in an elevated cell, so he is safe. For now.

I am increasingly learning to view life through the lens of a dog. Though I'm sure it can be done, it's difficult to overdose on optimism. An optimist sees stars in the dark, light through the clouds, and warmth in the cold. An optimist sees opportunity all around him. He goes looking for hope and finds it.

When Orville Kelly learned he had terminal cancer, he and his wife, Wanda, grieved together, prayed, and decided they should *play* about it. They threw a party for friends, and Orville announced, "This is a cancer party. I've been told I have terminal cancer. But my wife and I realized we are all terminal. We decided to start a new organization: MTC. Make Today Count. You are all charter members." Later, he said this.

> Looking back, I find it difficult to believe that I am the same person who blamed God for my cancer and who

doubted his existence. Perhaps, in my case, death made me aware of life. Each day I will accept not as another day closer to death, but as another day of life…I accept each day as a gift from God to be appreciated, enjoyed, and lived to its fullest.

I said goodbye to James and to Max. Mojo had already found a patch of sunlight streaming through a window and was sound asleep in it, dreaming of the spring day when the snowdrifts would be gone and she could stop awhile and chew the grass.

36

I Don't Have to Change You to Love You

When spring finally arrived, our pastor embarked on a sermon series about biblical prophecy. The first Sunday, he spoke about the rapture of the church, saying that Jesus would return one day to gather his children and whisk them skyward. Forgive my attention deficit issues, but I got to wondering how many of us would go, how many would stay, and what the rest of the service would look like for those left behind. I had no doubt about Ed Liever's destination. He was the youngest eighty-five-year-old I'd met. Ed loved telling others about Jesus, and he sang loud worship songs, calling them "amazing." Mr. Liever would blow the roof off this place.

But there were other unlikely candidates, though I won't name them. The preacher said there will be a trumpet blast preceding the rapture. Will it be a long blast, allowing people time to make things right? Or at least to grab hold of folks like Ed in hopes of hitching a ride? My mind didn't stop there. If the rapture happens while we're in church, I wondered, who will take care of our dog?

After the service, I voiced my deep theological question to a fellow dog owner. "The atheists are way ahead of you," he said. In the event of the rapture, they were graciously standing by to take care of my dog. Consoled by this, I ate lunch and then logged on. Sure enough, though the peace of mind would cost me dearly, he was right. So I sent off a note.

> Dear atheist friends! My Maltese–shih tzu dog is twelve. Does your lifetime guarantee last for the life of my pet or for my earthly life? I noticed that additional pets are fifteen

dollars each. Does this apply to goldfish, or would you consider a group price for a bowl of them? Thanks!

Mojo was scratching at the door. I opened it. She scooted past, covered in mud and guck and smelling of something foul. Much to her consternation, I swabbed her in lukewarm water and scrubbed her tracks from the floor. Then I checked my email. A good-humored reply was waiting.

"Hi, Phil! I sense a degree of enthusiasm that I could cut with a knife. Sorry, we cover your pet rescue contract for ten years. I recommend you flush those fish and save money." He took a few shots at Christians and then signed off, "Roger."

I responded quickly. "Thanks, Roger! I'm a follower of Jesus but not always a big fan of what I see in some of our churches. Christians are like manure—we do pretty well when we're spread out but don't always smell so good when you pile us together too long. All the best to you and yours!"

As the year went on, we continued to stay in touch. One day he admitted, "I've met some wonderful Christians through all of this. Next time you're on the East Coast I'm taking you out for lobster."

Roger called himself an anti-theist and loved to send me examples of Christians who had messed up. "You won't have to look far," I told him. "Just follow me around for a day." Roger admitted that he was angry, but I also found him thoughtful and intelligent.

We began comparing dogs (his was a small terrier), and I sent him a cartoon one day. Two fleas are walking along on the back of a dog between hairs the size of trees. One flea says to the other, "Sometimes I wonder if there really is a dog." I told Roger that I can't prove to him that there really is a God. But to reject the claims of Christianity, I would have to ignore some rather large hairs, some compelling clues and questions. Here were just a few.

Why is there something rather than nothing? Stephen Hawking wrote, "Almost everyone believes that the universe, and time itself, had a beginning." Nothing comes about without some outside cause. Call it one big mysterious bang if you will, but what caused that cause and the perfect calibration that followed?

Why the beauty in music, and these dogs, and artwork, and a sunset, and the longings they evoke in us? If we are products of accidental, meaningless, and random forces, why the sense that life and love mean so much?

How do you explain the life change God brings? Why, after a church sprang up within it, did Colombia's Bellavista, the most violent prison in Latin America, go from a murder a day to a murder a year?[1]

And what do you do with Jesus? Every historian agrees that the apostle Paul wrote his letters just fifteen to twenty years after Jesus's death. So how could Paul get away with writing his own eyewitness account and claiming that the risen Jesus appeared to more than five hundred people at once, most of whom were still alive? I can't get away with missing one minor detail in any of my books without receiving letters and phone calls.[2]

There have been thousands of messianic pretenders through the years. Only one had followers who went to their graves because they insisted he had been resurrected. Why would Jesus's disciples have done this unless they had seen him risen? No one dies for something he knows to be a lie. There is nothing private about a resurrection. Try faking one in your town.[3]

But in truth, Roger's greatest obstacle to faith was not God, but his responsibility to God, should he come to believe God exists. I told him that my dog shivers as I administer the dreaded bath, but a bath is not for her misery or because I am a vindictive master, but that she might enter a better world, one of health, freedom, and comfort. "Walking with God will not narrow your mind, your life, and your horizons," I wrote. "It will broaden them."

Mostly Roger disagreed when I talked like this, so we would circle back to talking about dogs, and I found myself getting rather doglike in my relationship with him. After all, my role wasn't to change him, but to be there, to care.

Without my dog I never would have met my friend Roger.

Never Overlook an Opportunity to Party

On the day my internal odometer flipped over to fifty, a younger friend called and sang the B.J. Thomas song, "Hair Plugs Keep Fallin' off My Head." I hung up on him. He called right back, laughing. "Hey," I groused, "I have a few rust spots and an overinflated tire, but I feel pretty chipper. And last I checked, no one had used the word 'chipper' in about forty years."

Even my dog was old. Moments before the phone call, thirteen-year-old Mojo fell asleep sitting on my lap, and were it not for my lightning reflexes, she would have hit the floor. I saved her life, but in doing so, I may have pulled some fat. I had reached the age where your muscles still don't have the good sense to lie dormant. Softball sounded like a great idea in the spring, but the summer was spent nursing Achilles tendons that felt as if they were being chewed on by a pack of rabid Pomeranians.

Two friends informed me that they didn't celebrate their fiftieth birthdays this year—just opted to ignore the doorbell and see if the visitor would go away. One reminded me of what the Bible says. "Outwardly we are wasting away."

"Finish the verse," I said, but he had already hung up.

The truth is, I felt pretty good for an old guy. I was able to get to the fridge and navigate most staircases. I exercised three times a week because it felt good when I stopped. And I rarely ate more than I could lift.

A primary inspiration in this aging process was my dog. A dog teaches you that today counts. That today is the oldest you've ever been and the youngest you'll ever be. Mojo inspired me daily with five secrets to dying young as old as I can.

Celebrate. I have yet to see this dog go a day without a celebration. Our son came home for the weekend, and she did somersaults. He filled her bowl to the brim—she did cartwheels. And why not celebrate? Without a doubt, I was happier at fifty than when I was a teenager. Life was hard back then. Each zit was leprosy, each weight room poster mocked me with what I could never be. I was happier at fifty than when I was the parent of three toddlers, though I loved them very much. They were low obedience and high maintenance. Life wasn't perfect at fifty, but decades earlier, I hadn't the time to do up my Velcro shoes. At fifty, I didn't miss student interviews, mortgage payments, or performance evaluations either. I could no longer hang from a tree swing by my feet as I once did, but I didn't mind. Such feats never took me very far anyway.

Abstain. An old dog avoids junk food like bread dough, chocolate, and grapes, so I was learning to keep my vices meager too. In fifth grade I was a pack-a-day smoker, but I quit the day I started. I still drank more soda at fifty than I should even though it contained all the goodness of radial tires. I was learning to enjoy salads if they were covered in cheese and to thirst for water with a squirt of lemon.

Play. Most evenings when I arrived home, this dog would get so excited that she'd hobble over to a toy basket, grab a stuffed bear, drop it at my feet, and stand there wagging everything she could wag. I would toss the bear the length of the kitchen and watch her saunter and pounce and return for more. May I never lose curiosity, playfulness, or the mischievous grin.

Pause. Our games of tossing the bear didn't last as long anymore. After three or four innings, she laid the bear at my feet and put her head on it. It's okay to pause. Looking back, you realize that people are rarely too busy to stop and tell you how busy they are. We wear our busyness like a badge of honor. Sometimes it's nice to pause.

Hope. An old dog can lose hope when the water bowl is empty as surely as I can lose hope looking in the mirror. Too much time mirrorgazing, and you discover that gravity doesn't tend to lift anything. But the last half of the Bible verse that my younger friend neglected to mention says this: "Inwardly we are being renewed day by day."[1] I must remember that this life is just the first chapter. The thought of eternity in heaven would make my hair stand on end if I had some.

Hope was bubbling to the surface more quickly than it did even a year earlier. And the thing about this hope is that it doesn't mean we're content to leave the world as it is. The great dog lover Clive Staples Lewis wrote, "It is since Christians have largely ceased to think of the other world that they have become so ineffective in this one." This hope beckons me to do something lasting while I'm here.

As I hit the fifty-year line, I could truly say for the first time in years that I loved life. I could stay up as late as I wanted now. Sometimes until eight p.m. My parents didn't tell me what to do anymore, though others had taken to doing so. That very week both the police and the doctor told me to slow down.[2]

38

You Can Find a Way out of Anything
Even Geezerhood

As Mojo's years increased, her zest for living showed no signs of dissipating. The tail no longer wagged her entire body, but she was just as excited to greet me each morning. You could see it in her eyes. One day when I badly needed it, she pounced on me after work, rolled over twice, buried her snout in my ear, and sneezed. Despite being unable to hear a thing at that point, I couldn't help but laugh.

People who work in the fields of psychiatry and humor hear from an extraordinarily high percentage of cranky people. Folks who have suppressed laughter for years. It is a perilous activity. A stifled laugh can back up all the way down your throat and spread to your thighs.

Just that morning a laugh suppressor called to say, "Callaway, I don't much like your sense of humor. What does laughing have to do with being a Christian? We're in the last days; this is hardly a time for laughter."

What would you say?

I replied, "Is that you, Dad?"

He didn't find this funny at all.

Each of us, regardless of occupation, is in danger of seeing the joy get systematically drained from our lives. For me, joyless living can be triggered by any of three dozen things. Criticism from others. Worry. Self-centeredness. Missing car keys. Bitterness. Any physical ailment, including a hangnail or an itch between my third and fourth toes. Chronic hiccups. Car trouble. Bad weather. And probably more than anything else, focusing on all that's wrong about the times in which I live, because that takes my focus off of living well in the times I'm given.

I once met a man who prided himself on how grumpy he was. He said he'd been evicted from restaurants, taxis, movie theaters, a football game, even a hair salon. He was impatient with lines, bitter with friends, critical of everyone, and generally an embarrassment to be around.

I resolved never to walk in his boot prints. The only way I would be evicted from a hair salon was for baldness. Then life happened. Stuff began to hurt. People began to irritate. And my natural reflex action was the upturned eyebrow, the downturned frown. Far too young, I officially entered geezerhood.

And then my dog showed me another path. Her unflappable optimism, more understandable in youth, stayed with her as her gait slowed, and the trait became even more endearing and inspiring to me. I am congenitally blind to so many of my own shortcomings, yet over and over this dog helped open my eyes.

Perhaps nowhere else is the virtue of crankiness more noticeably enshrined than in airports. I'm surprised they haven't erected a sign: Humor-Free Zone. I think if God wanted us to fly, he would have made it easier to get through security. Sure you'll find employees who make passengers smile, compliment travelers' luggage choices, and laugh when they get a chance, but they could be fired by Wednesday.

While being beeped through security, my wife was pulled aside. "Please step over here for a pat down, Miss," a uniformed gal instructed her. I leaned forward and asked, "May I give her one?" The appalled look I received made me wonder if I'd just yelled, "Bomb!"

Finally aboard, we discovered that a cat was sharing the row with us and one of the plane's engines needed doctoring. Travelers mumbled and groused, and I was one of them. Then, as the silver bird finally lifted off the ground, a little kid said loudly enough for at least half of us to hear, "Mommy! Look! We're flying!"

Most were too stressed to notice, but I couldn't help smiling. Like my dog, this kid looked through the mess and saw the masterpiece. "Are you kidding me? Look at us! Orville and Wilbur were amazing! We're flying!"

We all need a good dose of that kid, don't we?

We all need a good dose of our dogs.

Through the years Mojo left me without excuse when it came to knowing how to wake up each morning. Albert Einstein once said, "The problem with the speed of light is, it comes too early in the morning!" That is why my dog's fourfold technique should be bottled and sold on the open market.

First, she opens her eyes and scans the room, expecting to find something fantastic.

Second, she stretches and shakes. This gets her furry little body moving, alert and ready for whatever comes next.

Then she grins when she sees me. I don't know how else to describe it. Her ears lower. It's like her attitude reset button has been pushed. It's a grin, as noticeable as a dolphin's smile.

And finally, when we make our first connection of the day, her eyes close briefly with contentment, and her whole body seems to shout, "My master loves me."

At the dawn of a busy day that would see me fly fourteen hours, I flipped open my Bible and took time to read Psalm 104.

> O Lord my God, how great you are!…
>   You ride upon the wings of the wind…
> You placed the world on its foundation
>   so it would never be moved…
> Mountains rose and valleys sank
>   to the levels you decreed.
> Then you set a firm boundary for the seas,
>   so they would never again cover the earth…
> I will sing to the Lord as long as I live…

> May all my thoughts be pleasing to him,
>   for I rejoice in the LORD.

How can you start the day grumbling when you wake up like that? When you wake up expectant, ready, grateful, and grounded? You've got yourself a head start on the day—body, soul, spirit, and face.

And you haven't even gotten into the caffeine yet.

39

You *Can* Teach an Old Dog New Tricks

At the ripe old age of thirteen, in the space of a few short weeks, Mojo's hearing vanished like a teenager when the waiter brings the check. In hindsight, a good veterinarian may have prevented the early onset impairment, but I was slow to connect the dots. Toward the end of week two, I had my suspicions, and they were confirmed with a simple tuna test. No longer did the clink of a can opener bring her to the kitchen on the run. The nose brought her thirty seconds later, but nothing like her ears had done. And when I called, "Come, Moje!" there was no movement. She dozed on or just lay on the floor. Growing old ain't for pups.

Of the five primary senses, hearing ranks fourth or fifth for a dog. Smell is first, of course, followed by sight, taste, and hearing.

A dog won't last long in the wild without knowing who is sneaking up behind her, but a domesticated dog can do all right. Mojo was easily startled at first. A hand on her back and she jumped to her feet. And so we learned to get her attention by stamping gently on the floor nearby or by blowing lightly on her face. This she liked best. Her nose twitched, and she lifted her head.

Surprisingly little else changed with the loss of her hearing. We said goodbye to the quickness with which she jumped at the tantalizing words "Walk?" or "Food?" or "Car?" But she was still eager to stroll and eat and travel, and I continued to confide in her my secrets, knowing that you can tell a dog anything you want. Whether they pay you any notice is quite another matter.

They say you can't teach an old dog new tricks, but her lack of hearing did not affect her eagerness to learn, or at least to receive treats. Each night about ten p.m., in reward for her presleep rituals, I doled out bits of apricot or some delectable treasure when she did her tricks— jump, turn around, roll over, lie down, shake a paw, beg, high-five, and play dead. But with her hearing gone, she looked increasingly confused. So much so that she began to reconstruct the order of those tricks, eagerly performing a random assortment all on her own and then cocking her head as if to say, "Come on, that was close enough. Where's my reward?"

And so it was that I found myself signing for my dog. "Come" became a wave of the arm, "Stay" an upheld hand. Her bag of tricks soon morphed into amazingly accurate responses to my odd assortment of desperate hand signals, some of which mimicked her actions. She understood. She got it. I pawed the air. She begged. I drew a circle. She rolled over. Rather than a "Bang bang!" I went limp and hung my head, and in no time at all, she learned to play dead.

I began hiding treats around the house. She walked the house for close to an hour when I did this. Hoping. Looking. Sniffing.

Once again this dog taught me one of the keys to life and aging: If we look too long with regret on a closing door, we'll miss the one that's opening. A deaf dog is a more relaxed dog. She does not need to bark whenever the doorbell rings or recoil at each lightning bolt. New Year's Eve fireworks no longer gave her the shakes, and like a teenager, she could sleep longer without being wakened. All of life's battles have blessings too. But sometimes we have to go looking.

My mother had taken leave of more than her hearing by then, and she was finding life difficult. When we finally wrestled the car keys from her and drove her to a long-term care facility, the gal who coached me to go looking for blessings was finding it hard to find them herself.

But even there, blessings awaited us. Though Mom began to accuse me of stealing her money and divorcing my wife, she came alive whenever I put on some music or recited Bible verses. The children began to understand what it meant to care for those who couldn't care for themselves, and Mojo went along with it too, brightening the residents' lives—though I had to follow her around, for deaf dogs don't come when you call.

One lady in particular seemed as if she'd been locked up too long. Though pictures of her children and grandchildren were prominently displayed, none seemed to visit, and I have rarely seen a more gloomy face.

One night I discovered a small electric organ near Mom's room and helped her scooch on over to the middle of the bench. She had played the instrument in a dozen small churches throughout her life, so her fingers easily found the right keys. Nearby sat the gloomy lady, staring at nothing, but when Mom began to play, a smile stole like an Easter sunrise across this old gal's face. She began to sing in a quavery voice, low at first, "What a friend we have in Jesus, all our sins and griefs to bear. What a privilege to carry everything to God in prayer." Mom had found the foot pedals by then, so the volume reached a level that caused the lamp in an old chandelier to tremble, and the once gloomy lady tried to rise above it. "Can we find a friend so faithful, who will all our sorrows share? Jesus knows our every weakness; take it to the Lord in prayer."

I have heard better performances on some of the world's grand stages, but none have moved me like that beautiful song, performed by two lonely old saints, with the organ rumbling and the decibels rising to a level that caused even our deaf dog to sit up and take notice.

Don't Miss the Ocean
for the Waves

My favorite class in high school was without a doubt Communications 101, the brainchild of our creative English instructor, Mr. Al Bienert. One of the assignments was to prepare for a debate on a topic of our choosing. I chose, perhaps unwisely, to debate a passionate farm girl whom I fancied myself married to one day. Worse, the topic was "Which make better pets—cats or dogs?" I had no idea what a powder keg the subject was.

My opening comments were meant to be humorous. "I believe that God created cats to show that not everything on earth has a purpose." Perfectly kind-looking girls glared at me. Two threatened me with metal rulers. And then, right on cue, a friend brought Mojo One through the door. She came skidding toward me on the linoleum. Leaped joyfully. Licked my face and refused to leave my side. I was saved by the dog.

Following the debate, the entire class filed by, patting the dog, complimenting me on my eloquence. Sadly, the farm girl neither spoke to me nor acknowledged my presence after that. But I won the debate that day. Paws down.

My least favorite class was science, a class I flunked partly because a friend and I spent much of each lecture diagramming football plays. And partly because the farm girl's father taught the class. But I am fascinated by science now. I admire the dedication, knowledge, and commitment of scholars who study the knowable for the sheer joy of discovery, never once thinking, I am sure, of government grants.

Science is a gift to all of us. Without it, we'd still be steering donkeys and heating casseroles over fires.

Through the years I've read a dozen dog books, from novels to scientific tomes. I loved them all. From them I've learned fascinating things.

- The dog must always die during the closing chapter.
- We're just learning why dogs can see so well in the dark but often miss objects right before their noses.
- A dog's yawn is not a sign of boredom. It may indicate anxiety, timidity, or stress and is used by dogs to calm themselves and others.
- The average dog can detect a teaspoon of sugar diluted in two Olympic-sized pools full of water.
- Our auditory range is 20 hertz to 20 kilohertz. A dog can detect sounds up to 45 kilohertz.
- Though four Chihuahua heads will easily fit in a wolfhound's mouth, eye size varies only slightly between breeds.
- We should never test the Chihuahua–wolfhound theory.

With research on the increase and the findings ever changing, it strikes me that dogologists are just discovering the tip of the tail of an unimaginably complex creature. Not one of them is predicting that a hundred years from now, scientists will wake up and say, "Hey! That's it! We now know everything there is to discover about the dog. Let's study penguins." No, they will still be releasing new information about man's best friend.

In reading such findings, I was struck by the fact that sometimes brilliant researchers cannot see the ocean for the waves. To me it is unthinkable that a four-legged creature like this climbed out of the primordial ooze, untouched by a Creator. Isaac Newton, often regarded as the most influential scientist in history, once wrote, "In the absence of any other proof, the thumb alone would convince me of God's existence."

I think dogs are the gift of a loving God.

When I read that the human eyelid blinks four hundred million times during the average lifetime, and that it would take a Cray super-computer 100 years to simulate what occurs in the eye each second, I give thanks for science because it helps me marvel at the awesomeness of God. When I hear that we can see 2000 stars on a clear night but astronomers still haven't a clue how many there are, I am humbled. There are perhaps 100 billion stars in our little Milky Way galaxy alone—and billions of other galaxies.

The greatest minds of science have at times been humbled. And embarrassingly wrong. Until Copernicus showed up, most scientists believed the earth was the center of the universe. Pythagoras calculated that enough mirrors arranged correctly would allow you to write things on the moon (like "Hi, Mom," or "Γεια σου μαμά" in Greek). Then there was Nikola Tesla, who believed that he could build a death ray so powerful it could slice the earth in half. William Herschel, the first man to describe infrared radiation and to discover a planet with a telescope, believed the sun was a pleasant world populated by people with very large heads.

Of course that was then. Surely we're much wiser now. And I think we are. But soon after scientists encountered something called nuclear radiation, many folks assumed that something so miraculously energetic must be beneficial. So manufacturers of toothpaste and laxatives put radioactive thorium in their products.[1] In 1977 *Time* had a cover story, "How to Survive the Coming Ice Age." Asbestos wasn't banned until 1978. And I grew up in an era when smoking was good for you. If you weren't smoking in a mall, they would have you stand outside. Perky puffing physicians in lab coats were featured in magazine advertisements, puffing away. "More doctors smoke Camels than any other cigarette." You could even buy strawberry-flavored look-alike cigarettes for kids. Twelve to a pack, they were called "Just Like Dad." I think the surgeon general even smoked.

It's easy to laugh at ignorance displayed in the past, but do we really think future generations won't laugh at us?

"The wisdom of this world will always be out of date," said Tim Keller. "The things that well-educated intellectual people of one generation believe are almost always mercilessly ridiculed by the next generation of intellectuals…The experts of this age will look as stupid to your grandchildren as the experts of the last generation look to you."[2]

Can we really believe that our generation has written the final word on psychology or science or dogs? New studies are constantly unearthing the bad science in past studies. In the future, brilliant scientists will still be discredited. "All that is not eternal," wrote C.S. Lewis, "is eternally out of date."

I love science. Still, I dare not put my faith in a flimsy religion with a fickle priesthood, but in a God who is timeless and unchanging, a God who filled his creatures with meaning and purpose. And that even goes for cats too.

You Can Be the Kind of Person I Think You Are

Dating was nothing new for my daughter. Years ago Rachael began leaving our house once a month for dinner and a movie with the guy she loved—her dad. It wasn't for lack of alternatives. Boys proposed to her when she was three and four and twice when she was six.

In her teen years I rehearsed clever and witty things to say to the boys, threats involving staple guns. But I never had the heart while they stood there on our front steps, terrified, as if someone had already yelled, "Ready! Aim…"

"Why don't you go out with them?" I asked my daughter.

"Because I like dating you," she said. "You pay for everything."

Then along came Jordan, a tall, handsome dude who passed Rachael's first test: Our dog liked him. My wife liked him too. But I wasn't so sure. He was immensely helpful around the house, however. It was surprising the things I could get him to do for free. He cleaned the shed, repaired the dryer, mowed grass, and correctly assembled a barbecue, though a handful of parts were left over.

One day Jordan stammered, "I, uh, was going to talk to you about your daughter."

"And what," I asked, "were you going to say about her to me?"

"Uh, that I really like her."

I had those clever and witty threats ready. They were too good not to use. So while sharpening a knife, I informed him that if he broke her heart I would break some things he might need. I told him that nothing on earth matters more to me than this girl, that we've prayed for her every single day of her life—that she'd find a guy who doesn't talk about

God as much as he loves him. And I told him about the video surveil-lance units we've installed in every room. And in his car.

He chuckled nervously and said, "I'll be good to her."

The dog was sitting beside Jordan, looking up at him with admira-tion. And suddenly I felt a softening within. Acceptance is one of the greatest gifts a dog has to offer.

"I know you will," I said. "You can take her out, but you'll take the dog too."

He laughed nervously.

"I'm serious," I smiled. "This dog is a great judge of character. I've trained her to smell fear."

Just before Christmas, Jordan's enthusiasm for chores reached an all-time high, and one night while Ramona and I wrapped Christmas gifts, he tapped on our bedroom door and tiptoed in like a porcupine entering a balloon factory. Mojo looked up and wagged her tail.

"I was going to ask you about the, uh…(long pause)…marrying Rachael."

"Does she know about this?" was all that came to mind.

He grinned.

"Sit down," I said, stalling. Jordan sat on the bed, and Mojo jumped onto his lap. "You have the right to remain silent," I informed him. His grin widened. "Seriously, we've been watching you, and we like what we see. You're a gentleman. You make her laugh, and we've seen your love for Jesus. Rachael has made me very happy. She'll do the same for you if you let her. Just remember, I dated her first, you know."

As Mojo licked his hand, I asked a few simple questions. Why would you like to marry her? Will you be stronger together than apart? How do you plan to encourage her gifts? Are you honoring her now? What will you do if marriage doesn't turn out the way you planned? Easy stuff.

Jordan spluttered a little, so I suggested we talk about these things during the seven years he would spend raising cattle for me. He laughed and scratched the dog's ears. "We share some stuff in common," he said.

"That's good. That's important in a marriage."

"No, I mean Mojo and me." Jordan seemed a little more relaxed.

"Like what?"

"We both like taking Rachael for walks and sitting close to her on the couch."

"Ah, you have a great sense of humor."

"I think I'll need it," he said. We laughed, and Mojo followed him from the room, unaware that she'd played a starring role in this romance. According to Rachael, she had. "The dog likes Jordan more than me," she said one day. And I took some comfort in that.

Stories abound of dogs sniffing out people of ill character. Some are likely true. Dogologists confirm that fear smells to a dog. Pheromones are involuntarily produced when we are alarmed, enabling dogs to smell our apprehension and fright. Dogs are trained to bring down fleeing criminals based on both the odor of a human and the smell of fear.

Three days after Christmas, the fearless Jordan Culp produced a sparkling diamond set in gold, got down on one knee, and popped the question. "Will you marry me?" It wasn't the first time she'd been asked, but this time Rachael broke down and cried. And said yes.

We couldn't have been happier for them. But like a cassette tape plugged into a Blu-ray machine, we began to realize that life was changing fast. Our two sons, once so dependent on us, had flown the coop. Now our daughter would too. One night when she was out, I stood in her empty room, looking at the Winnie the Pooh border we'd put up together. And I got a little emotional. The dog had jumped on her bed where she would sleep until Rachael was gone. Mojo lay down and looked at me. "Give thanks for what you have," she seemed to say. And so I did. I gave thanks for kids and dogs and all the memories. The truth is, this new chapter would see us praying more and fighting the urge to offer unsolicited advice.

When Jordan arrived back that evening, I asked him, "May I have your permission to date her when you're married?"

"If you take the dog," he said.

Sometimes we watched them in the car talking about their June wedding (the picture was quite clear from our newfangled surveillance cameras). They were planning a lavish catered affair, but I thought we should have a backyard potluck. A through E—bring a hot dish. F through M, salads. N through Z would be toasters. I hadn't mentioned it to Rachael, but surely she would leave that decision up to me.

After all, I'm the dad. I pay for everything.

It's Okay to Ask

When our son came home from camp one summer, I asked him, "Did you get homesick?"

"Yep," he replied. "All the kids who have dogs did."

Dogs. Why do we love them? My friend Vance prefers to live without a dog. He picks his own food off the floor and walks himself. He uses an alarm clock. His pants are cleaner, his yard is less blotchy, and his windows seldom have sneeze marks. But I prefer the companionship of this four-footed creature for so many reasons. One of them is this: Dogs are good listeners. Or at least they appear to be. More than almost any other trait, a dog's ability to sit and listen sets it apart from every other animal. I think I'll market a T-shirt: "My dog thinks I'm brilliant." It's true. I can talk about anything at all and she'll look my way and blink, her eyes filled with admiration. Dogs listen. And when we're hurting they seem to have an innate sense that we need their presence. We need their silence. We need companionship.

Through the years I had learned some things the hard way.

- Never light the barbecue before opening the lid.
- You can safely ignore the warning labels on everything but superglue.
- Don't fry bacon with your shirt off.
- Laughter is not the best medicine for cracked ribs.

But now my dog would teach me far more valuable lessons during the most difficult year of our lives.

In March a knee injury sidelined my golf game. That wasn't so bad.

My daughter was moving overseas. That was a cakewalk. But when a friend's wife betrayed him, it knocked the stuffing out of me. Then my wife's mother died. Then her stepdad. Next her sister Cynthia passed away after two decades with Huntington's disease. Another sister, Miriam, was down to forty-seven pounds with this dreadful disease before succumbing. Both left behind faithful husbands, kids, and grandbabies who loved them very much.

Add to that a diagnosis that left my best friend and traveling companion, Lauren, and his wife stunned. "Colon cancer. It's gone to the bone." The chemo altered his taste buds, and his beloved five-cup-a-day coffee habit was the first to go. His insanely active border collie, Kelly, had always been a handful, so with Lauren's energy gone, he was forced to give the dog to his grown son. We loved hitting golf balls together. Kelly loved retrieving them. With Lauren on crutches, that was gone too. "It wasn't entirely selfless, giving Kelly away," he smiled one day. "The dog was driving me nuts." We still found things to laugh about, but each time we got together, his rapid deterioration was noticeable, and with all the other deaths, it was like someone was pinching my oxygen tube.

They don't have a high school class that prepares you for these things. Or seminary, for that matter.

I knew that many were dealing with far greater pain and that I had much to be thankful for. Still, I didn't want anyone telling me that because they may not have appreciated my response. Some redneck said, "If the world didn't suck we'd all fall off," and when I heard those words, I thought, *He's right. At some point life hurts for all of us.*

Mojo seemed to know this. She couldn't jump on my lap anymore, but with increased regularity she pawed at my knees, asking for a piece of whatever I was eating or just a place to sit and comfort me. As she sat there, I voiced some of my questions out loud. "Why, God? Why all at once? Why not spread it out a little? Why not step in and rid the world of these horrid diseases? Why not make it right?"

Asking questions is okay. God doesn't say, "Uh-oh! That Callaway guy is asking questions again. Whatever will we do?" God is big enough. And even if we never hear the answers in this life, we ask because we care, because we hurt, because we have the courage to ask them. And any father knows that when a child asks, it sure beats silence.

I asked other questions too. "Why do some comforters only make it worse?" I wasn't comparing myself to Job, but when one of my would-be comforters said, "I guess God needed them more than you did," I had nothing to say. I had no idea how to relate to such a thought, much less respond to it. I didn't smite this guy between the shoulder blades, but I wanted to.

A few other bumper-sticker clichés were offered to us. "It was their time." Again, I have no idea how this helps. They were gone. We missed them. Yes, we believed we would see them again one day, but there's a season for everything, and this was the season to miss their laughter and encouragement.

Someone else said, "God won't give you more than you can handle." And I told Mojo with no uncertainty that this may look good on a bumper sticker, but it wasn't in the Bible. I looked. First Corinthians 10:13 assures us that God won't allow us to be *tempted* beyond what we're able to bear. He'll provide a way of escape. Paul was talking about temptation, not suffering. We can flee temptation. We can't flee suffering.

Looking at a fifteen-year-old dog who had just turned three circles and slumped on my lap, I said out loud, "I think we get more than we can handle sometimes. I think it causes us to turn to the only One big enough to help us carry it." The apostle Paul once admitted that he was so utterly burdened, he despaired of life itself. That's when he learned to rely not on himself, but on God.[1] We can't run from suffering, but we can turn to God in it.

One night I talked with longtime friends and dog lovers Conrad and Marylynne. They said they were sorry. Like my dog, they listened. I thought I saw tears in their eyes. We got to laughing about great memories. Crazy stuff we'd done. The laughter felt so good.

I picked up a handmade card they had given me. It was more meaningful than any you can buy in a store. Written on the front by friends who have hurt too were these life-giving words from Psalm 91:

This I declare about the LORD:
   He alone is my refuge, my place of safety;
he is my God, and I trust him.

In time the questions would turn into thanksgiving. For memories of these faithful lives. For friends who listen. And dogs who teach us that it's okay to ask.

43

It's Noisy Out There

Be Careful Which Voices You Listen To

Three days and Rachael was to leave with her new husband for Germany. The house was a flurry of activity—packing, arguing about what was being packed, asking forgiveness, packing again. They were to work as dorm parents to teenage boys at a school called Black Forest Academy. I could only blame myself, I suppose. Traveling with their dad gave our kids a sweet taste of adventure that they couldn't wash from their mouths, and now they had each ventured overseas at some point with the goal of serving others. You want the children to be an improvement on you, but when it happens you're startled.

During Rachael's last few days of living nearby, I began to notice something. At each opportunity she stopped by to take the dog with her—to the grocery store, to a baseball game, for doggie sleepovers. As she sat on our couch one August night, she held the dog close to her face, as if she were saying goodbye. I suppose she was. You don't leave a fifteen-year-old dog for two years expecting a grand reunion one day.

I sat on the sofa beside her and rested my head on her shoulder. "Teenage boys?" I joked. "Have you lost your minds?"

She was massaging the dog's shoulders. "Do mine," I said.

"Ah, Daddy." Into her twenties and still she called me this.

"I don't know if you remember, but when you were pretty small, I came around the corner of the house one day, and you were standing there with your hands on your hips, yelling at a neighbor kid."

"Who?"

"It doesn't matter. He's grown up since then."

"Why was I yelling?"

"Well, he had a stick and was about to hit Mojo with it."

She looked down at the dog and nuzzled closer. "Ah, Moje," she said.

"I don't know what was going on in the kid's life or what his problem was, but you told him to back up and leave the dog alone. I didn't have to say a thing."

"Good for me," she smiled.

"That was a tough year for you."

"Was that the year Miss—?"

"Yep," I interrupted.

Silence. Until September of that year, Rachael had believed in dragons and fairies and Aslan. She would whisper to rocks and leaves as she walked to school, daydreaming about faraway lands. In October she experienced her first crush, sneaking glances across the room, willing the boy to notice her. And from her desk she traveled to other worlds, where she could escape from the glare of a teacher.

The dog had curled up between us now. Rachael said, "I learned that year that I was stupid. She would stop class to ask if I was daydreaming again. She was smart. I wasn't. So I believed her. I remember the day I suddenly realized how stupid I must be. She stood over me and said, 'Count your folders.' I was so nervous I counted nine. I was wrong. 'You can't even count to ten?' she asked for all the class to hear."

The tears had come to Rachael's eyes. And to mine. How I wished I could have known, could have done something. The girl was good at counting now. She could write stories I wanted to read.

"I'm so sorry, Rachael. But you had other teachers. Tell me about them."

"I had great teachers. But her voice is still the loudest. She told me I couldn't read and sent me to Mr. Massey's office for remedial reading during lunch." She brightened. "He encouraged me. Made me laugh. Shared his veggies with me. For an hour the fear was gone. He was kind and funny, and I learned something. I learned that my teacher was wrong."

"Yes, she was," I said. "Please remember that when you hear her voice. You are my beloved daughter, and you're a daughter of the King. And remember to forgive her each time she pops into your head. I've heard some of those voices too."

The dog was softly whistling through one nostril now like a faraway train. We laughed.

"Know why we're going to live with a dorm full of boys?" she said, plugging the dog's nostrils with a finger.

"Why?"

Mojo snorted and sat up.

"Well, Mr. Massey told me I was a good reader. And I believed him. Last year I read more than a hundred books. Novels. Classics. Missionary biographies. When I read the book *Girl Soldier*…have you read it, Daddy?"

"No, but I guess I better."

"Do. It's about a young girl in Uganda who is kidnapped along with a hundred other girls to be 'wives' to officers in the Lord's Resistance Army. It's the story of how God helped and delivered her. After reading that, Jordan and I watched *Les Miserables*, and I couldn't stop thinking about the young, sweet girl Fantine, who was forced into prostitution to save her daughter. I wanted to do something to help. So I started praying that God would give me a chance to teach young men how to honor women. I guess this is the answer."

"You're gonna make me cry," I said. "You know, followers of Jesus have always been pioneers in compassionate care. Hospitals. Leprosariums. Orphanages. I haven't found the Bertrand Russell Children's Home yet. Or the Voltaire Hospital."

Rachael was softly scratching under Mojo's collar.

"Remember the little girl in the movie *The Help*?" I asked. "You is kind, Rachael. You is smart, you is important. You've always had a soft spot for the underdog. I guess I didn't understand quite why until today."

"Thanks, Daddy," she said. Then she put a finger over Mojo's nose. The dog was whistling again.

44

It's Never Too Late
to Think of Others

I was leaving on a flight somewhere, and I called Lauren. His cancer was spreading quickly now, and I wondered if I'd see him again this side of heaven.

He told me that new treatments were on the way, and we both brightened a little at thoughts of rekindled hope. "I'm kinda worried though," he admitted. "About Caroline. About the kids. It's the hardest thing about all this. I'll miss the grandchildren." Then he did what he always did—he asked me how I was doing.

Just weeks after his cancer diagnosis, we had said goodbye to our families and dogs and flown to an eastern city together where I was to speak. I reminded Lauren of our adventure and the laughter. A flight attendant was a friend from years ago who bumped us up to first class, complete with vibrating seats and our choice of appetizers, entrées, and desserts. Lauren has always been cheaper than a three-dollar steak, so this was like buying jeans at Salvation Army and finding a hundred bucks in the pocket.

When we rented a car, the gal typing in our info suddenly cursed, using Jesus's name. Lauren leaned forward and said in his wide-eyed, winsome way, "You're a Christian too?" She couldn't stop laughing. So she handed us keys to a triple upgrade Mustang convertible.

Lauren loved baseball as much as I, so we drove to a major league stadium where a father and son leaving the ballpark handed us two tickets. Row 10. Behind the dugout.

"Do you remember when we parked?" Lauren laughed. "A guy waved us into his space and handed us his receipt. Free parking. I'll never forget it. It was a cheapskate's dream."

I said, "I wonder if maybe it was God's way of saying, 'I know you're cheap. I'm extravagant. I know you hurt. I hurt too. Trust me. I'll take care of you all the way home. Caroline and the kids too.'"

Lauren was quiet.

I once asked him about dealing with cancer. He put a little thought into it and then sat down and wrote these words for me.

> Even though I may not choose cancer or even like what I'm going through, even though I tend to feel sorry for myself way too often, there are others in the family going through Huntington's disease and experiencing suffering I can't imagine. God is faithful and merciful beyond what I deserve. How do I know? He hung on the cross for me. He knows what suffering is, and he walks with me through mine even though I can't always tell he's there. Maybe someday he will help me to count it all joy. I can't make that claim yet. But someday. They call cancer the Big C. The Big C for me is Christ. So I hope to never lose sight of the goal. Something that gets lost in my little world all too often—Jesus is to be glorified in me. May I make it so.

"Do you have any regrets?" I don't know why I asked it, but I did.

"Maybe we should have golfed more. And, well…I wish I'd been in full-time ministry like you."

"Oh, man," I said. "You have been. I've seen how you are around the people you work with. They know you love Jesus. They know you love them too."

Most of our phone conversations included some jokes. Usually Lauren did the telling, trying out a variety of accents—anything to make me laugh. This time he told me of a forty-year-old lady in a hospital. Just before being operated on she asked God, "Am I going to die?"

She heard a voice. "No. You will live another forty years."

Upon coming out of surgery she was so excited at her new lease on life that she got a face-lift, liposuction, nips and tucks, and a complete makeover. A week later she was hit by a bus. Standing before her Maker, she exclaimed, "I thought you said I had another forty years."

He replied, "Oh! I'm terribly sorry. I didn't recognize you."

I think we laughed so hard because we knew our Maker. We knew he would recognize us and one day welcome us home.

Even Lauren's dog Kelly got in on the act. When his son brought the dog, she sensed that something was wrong. Kelly would come over and rest her head on Lauren's knee sometimes, looking up, slowly wagging her tail.

I talked with Lauren once more on that trip, and then his wife, Caroline, called with the news. "He broke both legs and an arm. I found him in the bathroom. He's in hospice care. The doctor says he only has a few days left."

It was the first time I had visited Lauren without my dog. As he came in and out of consciousness, I sat beside his bed and talked with his fellow workers, who timidly tapped at the door hoping to see him. Tears came as they talked of this gentle giant whom his employer kept trying to promote with promises of more notoriety and more money in a larger city. But Lauren wanted to live near family and friends.

"He loved God, you know," one coworker told me.

"Yes," I smiled. "And he loved you too. I heard him pray for you."

We celebrated his thirty-fifth wedding anniversary as his wife combed his hair and reassured him of her love.

"It'll be okay," were the last words I heard him say. His eyes brightened as he said it. Caroline smiled.

The next day he was gone.

"See You Later" Always Trumps "Goodbye"

There is nothing quite like a Christian funeral. "See you later" always trumps "Goodbye." I was asked to say a few things at Lauren's memorial. And so I did.

"This week just about everything reminded me of Lauren. I never drink coffee. This week I guzzled two cups. And thought of him. If Starbucks offered an IV drip, he would have been first in line. I miss him so much I almost had a Costco hot dog, but when we ate them he'd often say, 'These things will kill you,' so I abstained.

"I golfed with my sons this week, and we talked of Lauren. He loved the game because it offered him hope. Hope that with the next shot a miracle would occur and the ball would go straight. It happened twice for him. Which shows you just how much God loved Lauren. He only turned water into wine once.

"Lauren seldom met a child he couldn't encourage, a dog he couldn't love, a room he couldn't brighten, a movie he couldn't sleep through, or a golf club he couldn't throw. For twenty-five years he took a self-less interest in our kids. I don't know of anyone, outside our dog, who has modeled selflessness more accurately. Our youngest said, 'He teased me when I was a kid, became my friend when I lived with him while attending university, and was like a brother when I was going through tough stuff.' Lauren was like a second dad to him, maybe better, because he wasn't so uptight.

"Our daughter, Rachael, wrote from Germany. 'Uncle Lauren is the reason I like the smell of coffee—not for coffee's sake, but the smell of coffee in our home meant he was there, and I loved our home even more when he was in it. He asked me when I was a little girl if I'd like to stay with him and be his daughter, and I remember pausing to seriously consider it. Uncle Lauren made me feel like I was the most important person in the world, totally loved, just for being me. My husband, Jordan, will miss being called Jarod, Jabez, and Jehu, and I will miss one of the most Christlike men I've ever known.'

"Six out of ten times when he phoned, he'd mimic some celebrity and get me laughing. And when a trip grew dull, he would narrate it, making up names for people on a bus or plane. He was refreshingly real. We watched some pretty juvenile movies together. I have seen him laugh so hard I didn't think he'd recover. Even in the face of great difficulty, God gave him great joy.

"Yesterday a friend of mine who is here handed me this letter. He said, 'You read it. There's no way I'll make it through.'

> A few years ago, as a result of a series of exceedingly bad choices, I ended up in prison, hours from home and family. As I languished in my cell, a letter arrived. It said, "I'm Phil's brother-in-law. I'd like to come visit you." It had his phone number and an offer to pay for the call if it cost anything.
>
> To visit me would take great persistence. First he had to call the institution and hand-deliver a letter requesting to be put on a visitor's list. Next he was subject to background checks. Finally one Sunday afternoon I was summoned for the first of several visits with Lauren. He wasn't there to counsel, exhort, admonish, or judge me. He had no agenda. He just wanted to be my friend. We talked about church, family, and life. I forgot about the dismal day-to-day existence that had befallen me and was reminded that there are people who are still willing to be the hands and feet of Jesus.
>
> Once, without him knowing it happened, three cancer pills fell from his pocket. A guard came to interrogate me, thinking Lauren was a drug dealer. During another visit he

apologized for the length of time between visits because he took a little longer to rebound from his last round of chemotherapy. I wonder if he saw my eyes fill with tears.

I don't know if Lauren realized what his selflessness meant. His quiet and faithful presence was profound. Here was a man I hardly knew, in the midst of his own personal battle, demonstrating love to me—a man who had seriously screwed up his life. I'm convinced that if this was the kind of pure religion that people saw, our churches would not be able to contain the number of people flocking to their doors. I can still see Lauren sitting there waiting for me in the visitation lounge on those Sunday afternoons. Almost as if Jesus himself came to prison.

"We loved much of the same music, Lauren and I. You should have seen us in rental cars, the music turned up, pretending we had hair. One of the last CDs he bought was from Bruce Carroll. He loved one of the songs about how God never knew a sinner he couldn't love or a broken heart he couldn't mend. I wrote Bruce this week to tell him how much that song meant to Lauren. He quickly responded with this— 'I'm so sorry about Lauren. Death isn't final, my friend.'

"His coworkers and folk at the coffee shop loved him. I think it's partly because the world would rather see a sermon than hear one. This week I've been thinking about my selfless friend. I'd like to be a lot more like him. That way I'll be a little more like Jesus."

The Best Vitamin for Friendship Is B1

never expected this dog to teach me about such a wide spectrum of life. Like parenting, for instance. From a dog you learn that things will get messy, noisy, and covered in guck. Expect it. Embrace it. Relax about it. I've noticed that the most ineffective parents are the uptight ones. Tense. Anxious. Furrowed. With our first child, we had all the parenting books arranged alphabetically. We bathed this wriggly little guy each night, videotaped his every "Ga-ga," and consulted medical books at the first sign of hiccups. By the time our third came along, we had parked that helicopter. We were so exhausted that we let our youngest chew and rearrange the parenting books and bathe himself in mud puddles. I think that perhaps maybe somewhere we have a couple of pictures to prove the boy did just fine. (So did our first, by the grace of God.)

If I had to parent again, I wouldn't be so uptight about it. I would pray more and not sweat or fret about spilled root beer, scratched cars, or enrolling my kid in every soccer/football/chess/sumo competition within forty miles. I would celebrate grass stains, and when Rachael buried the remote control in the sandbox, I would give her a high-five and leave it there a day or two. I can't look at my dog without her saying almost audibly, "Chill. Loosen up. Relax."

This dog taught me other things too. She taught me to walk outdoors, to sit a little longer by a crackling fire, to stay in a tent rather than a five-star hotel, and to stretch out a walk by stopping and talking to people I wouldn't otherwise talk to.

This dog taught me perspective. That I don't have to understand everything to be happy. That I should live life right now. And a bad hair day? Who really cares? In fact, when people get ahold of you and fix your hair, you just rub your head into the carpet, and you'll be fine. And when someone blames you for gas, don't dignify it with a response.

This dog taught me that there is a time for making your point with great fanfare, but mostly silence is golden. This dog taught me to sleep, eat, and play. To judge not. To be tolerant. Except in the face of evil.

Two doors down lived Sidney, Mojo's sniffmate. Life dealt Sidney the meanest of cards when his parents—a terrier and a dachshund—got together and said, "Hey! Let's start a family!" Sidney's belly rode an inch above the grass, his eyes drooped, one black ear shot straight up, the other straight out. Sidney's speech was impaired too. His bark sounded like people's names—Raul! Mark! Ralph! He didn't care. Nor did Mojo. Each day Sidney waddled to our doorstep and let out a muted "Warroo!" Mojo sprinted to the door, and the two of them danced and cavorted and sniffed. Mojo taught us about acceptance. That when a friend calls, you drop everything and go. Sidney taught us that the best vitamin for friendship is B1.

This dog taught me to forgive more easily. To keep short accounts.

She taught me that life will smack you, but you get back up, wag your tail, and move forward one step at a time. That sometimes you should roll on your back and kick your legs in the air just for fun.

Mojo taught me the virtue of persistence. That if you stare at someone long enough, they will let you in or feed you some cheese.

She taught me to stop looking for perfection. That people are like pizzas. Most are marvelous, but sometimes they come with anchovies. So focus on the good stuff and roll with the rest.

She taught me to stop pretending. That what you see is what you get. That if I'm not the sort of friend they're looking for, I'd better save them some time in making a decision. At some point I'll have to be myself anyway. No matter how friendly I am, not everyone will be my friend. A dog may be a lot of things, but he's no hypocrite, so be who you is, because if you ain't who you is, you is who you ain't.

This dog taught me to walk after eating, to move on after mistakes. When you mess up, apologize and refuse to lug it around with you.

This dog taught me that eating too much can cause problems. That we should rarely eat an entire cheesecake all by ourselves. And when we do, sit there and look cute. A cute face can cover a multitude of sins.

This dog taught me to protect those I love. That when you're excited, it's okay to show it. That when you love someone, you should say so.

No matter how wonderful a dog is, there is always a mess to clean up. That's okay. That's life.

And it's hard to stay mad when something cute licks your nose.

In her fifteenth year, Mojo met me at the door, and though she couldn't jump as high, she put everything into each greeting. And I thought to myself, *I get it. Thanks for showing me. From now on—with the exception of salesmen—no one gets out of this house without a hug. And no one leaves here on a trip without an arm around their shoulder and a prayer for their safety.*

Like my dog, I will enjoy small pleasures. And the people in my life will never doubt that I loved them. And when possible, I will take pictures to prove that it happened.

47

You Can Grow Old Without Getting Ugly

Years ago an old dog was abandoned on a country road many miles from home. In his search for food and affection, he happened upon a little country church. The minister patted the dog's head and put food in a dish and water in a bowl. A nearby family adopted him, but he could often be found at the church, where he knew he'd be nurtured and fed.

My parents' closest friends, Fred and Martha Meisner, faithfully attended the same church. Their daughter Kathy told me the story and added, "I go to church now partly because a dog helped get me there. I couldn't wait to see him each Sunday." The dog waddled through the parking lot, warmly greeting everyone when they arrived. "It was too old to jump all over us. It just wagged its tail as if to say, 'Good to see you...what took you so long to come back?'"

The dogs of my childhood did nothing to get me to church. If anything, they hindered the process. But my parents did not. What I saw in their lives made me want what they had. Both had come to faith in Jesus in their teen years, undergoing remarkable transformations. Dad was forty when I was born, so he'd had a few decades to figure out what was worth living and dying for.

I credit him with my sense of humor. He'd seen long-faced Christianity and wanted no part of it. Dad took God seriously—himself, not so much. His was a home filled with the laughter of the forgiven, a joy that found a way to trump depression and the loss of a child.

A ten-pound canine didn't hurt either. My father loved the dog. As Dad slipped further and further into the valley of Alzheimer's, he continued to brighten when I arrived to visit, but he positively beamed when I brought the dog. Unable to carry a thought long enough to complete a sentence, Dad just sat on his recliner, studying the dog's face and patting her. "Blessing," he said, as Mojo closed her eyes and leaned against him.

A nurse met with me to discuss care and resuscitation protocol, and I stammered my way through it. Dad had always seemed immortal to me, but the years sneak up on you like that pointy-headed classmate you thought you could beat in a relay race.

"We really like him here," said the nurse, not bothering to wipe a tear from her eye. "He's so kind. And he makes us laugh." I thanked her and stood to leave. "Oh, and you can bring your dog anytime." She bent down and patted Mojo. "We don't like all the dogs. We like this one."

Conversations with my father were lopsided affairs now. I talked about weather and the kids and the view from his window. I recounted some of Dad's childhood pranks for him. He smiled and tried out a few words but then gave up. I reminded him of the words he had spoken to me so often—"It'll look better in the morning. No eye has seen and no ear has heard what God has prepared for those who love him." Mojo just parked herself on his lap as if there was no place she'd rather be. Accounting for dog years, the two were about the same age.

Lunch arrived on a tray. "I found an extra one for you," the nurse said to me. I thanked her for the soup and sandwich, and thanked God for small mercies. Like the fact that Dad hadn't changed as much as many patients do when staring down the barrel of this dread condition. "He's been playing peek-a-boo with us," she laughed. "Good night, Bill." She kissed him gently on the cheek. Later that night I would find him holding hands with a complete stranger, a woman who had been single all her life.

A friend has this hanging in his entryway: "Everyone brings joy to this house. Some when they arrive and some when they depart." And it's true—of both dogs and people, I suppose. You meet two kinds of people on this earth. Some bring happiness wherever they go, and others bring happiness *whenever* they go. Dad fit snuggly into the first category. For all his failures and shortcomings, he was like that old dog in the church parking lot. Like Mojo in the nursing home. Dad didn't really think about it; he just brought joy along. It was never an act for him.

That was the last time the dog would sit on that welcoming lap and lean into that gentle caress. Two weeks later on a Friday, my brother Tim spent the night on a recliner beside my father's bed. Early in the morning as Tim watched the sunrise, Dad stopped breathing. The sun painted two shafts of light on the wall in the shape of a cross. No more tears. No more Alzheimer's. Dad was home free.

48

I'm Rescued, Adopted, and Spoiled

Most of us would like to be a little more like our dogs. Apart from being covered in hair, of course. We'd like to sleep half the day and have someone else clean up after us and then bring us dinner for free.

When we asked folks what they loved about their dogs, the answers went far beyond laziness. Fifty-six percent of our surveyed dog lovers used the word "companionship." Thirty-five percent listed unconditional love. Three percent said, "They get us out for walks."

When asked what their dogs had taught them, many indicated that they'd like less stress and more play, fewer commitments and more fun.

"I'd like to make up more quickly after a fight," admitted June.

"When presented with an opportunity to get outside, I jump at it," said Ken.

"I envy my dog's ability to fall asleep almost anywhere," wrote Prentice. Terry said her dog had taught her to stop fussing so much about her hair each morning.

Others admired a dog's ability to be ecstatic about little things. Like a soft pillow and a caterpillar. To stand their ground even if it looks like they will lose. To be a good judge of character. To be still. Unconcerned. Trusting. Cuddly. To live now. To love without condition. To accept people the way they are. That if you can find someone to scratch your belly, you're rich.

"I would like to be as attentive, loving, and obedient to God as my dog is to me," wrote Lynn.

"I would like to be so persuasive with my eyes," said Caroline.

"I stepped on my dog's paw this morning, and she limped for a few minutes," wrote David. "Now she is lying by my side, the consummate forgiver. I'd like to forgive like that. I'd like to be more like my dog."

When we asked, "What has your dog taught you about God?" just over two-thirds of the responses had to do with God's love. "She gives me the feeling I am loved and never alone."

"We rescued our sheltie from a horribly abusive situation," wrote Rebecca. "He is a daily reminder that God rescued me and adopted me. We love this little dog. How much more God must love us."

Others said, "Whenever I think God has forgotten me, I think of my dog and know he hasn't."

"God has given us dogs to remind us that he loves us. All we need to do is come to him."

"Always there."

"Loves me no matter what."

"Forgives."

"Has the patience of a saint."

"My dog's faithfulness makes me think of God."

"Max reminds me that God will always care for me—even when I rip up tomato plants."

"God is good. He gave me a dog to love and care for."

"God is loyal and attentive."

"He has made all things beautiful."

"When I mess up and ask forgiveness, he immediately forgets about it."

"He wants to enrich our lives. After all, he gave us animals to enjoy."

"Just as I take care of my dog's needs, God takes care of mine."

"God loves animals enough to give them their own unique personalities and qualities."

"I've struggled to be patient in prayer. My pug reminds me of how hard it is to communicate when we don't speak the same language. But we find a way."

"Love isn't earned, it's just given."

"How do I know that God will always love me, no matter how badly

I mess up or how often I make the same mistake? The Bible tells me so. So does my dog."

"Both my dogs were rescue dogs, and both were strays. Every summer we enjoyed a road trip with them. We traveled together on planes, ferries, and trams. One day I was reminding our first dog, Abby, that she was once an abandoned mutt, but now she is rescued and spoiled, loved, provided for, and taken on great adventures. I started to tear up as I realized that is exactly what God did for me."

"Coda has taught me about God's compassion," wrote Marsha Lyn. "We must seem like such clumsy puppies to him, always getting ourselves into trouble, having to be taught the same lessons over and over and over again. Yet he never gives up on us."

Our dogs teach us lessons beyond compare if we sit up and pay attention. I grew up thinking that when it came to faith, I could just follow the rules, and I would measure up. This made me prideful, self-centered, and judgmental. God became a distant deity to be feared, one I could appease only by my good works. When I encountered the biblical concept of grace, it blew me away. I get what I can't buy, earn, or deserve? Yes. Jesus would rather die than live without me.

The concept was cemented when this dog entered our house. I don't think I'm exaggerating when I say that Mojo brought God closer. She showed me that I am loved for who I am, not for what I can do or say or bring. She taught me a lesson in grace—God likes me. He wants to hang out with me, even when I've chewed a shoe or destroyed a lawn chair. Who wouldn't adore a God like that?

This dog's love is helping me understand my Master's love a little better. Like a dog in the pet shop window, I can't wait until my Master shows up to bring me home.

49

I Can Find My Way
Home from Anywhere

Adog teaches us much about life. Death too. Those who don't want to think of death should buy themselves a sea turtle. They outlive you. But they don't register on the cuddly scale. Inviting a tiny fur-ball into your home, fully aware of its life expectancy, accomplishes many things. Few are more valuable than bringing us face-to-face with the shortness of time.

In ninth grade I began reading *Where the Red Fern Grows,* drawn in by this winsome tale of a pair of redbone coonhounds and the love of a boy named Billy, who worked two years to earn enough money to purchase them. With his new puppies in tow, Billy came to a sycamore tree where the names Dan and Ann had been carved inside a heart. He named the puppies after the carving, and as the story moved along they stole his heart. Mine too.

When in the end Old Dan dies saving Billy from a mountain lion, and Little Ann is so sad that she loses her will to live and crawls onto Old Dan's grave and dies, well, let me just say that up until then I had a very happy childhood.

And when the boy visits his dogs' graves and finds a giant red fern growing between them, something that according to Indian legend, only an angel can plant, I came apart.

I was lying on the sofa, and I remember despairing because my brother, Tim, and my sister, Ruth, were in the kitchen. It seemed impossible for me to slink past without them noticing the tears racing toward my chin. So I turned to the wall and pretended to sleep, as much as you can when you are a blubbering mess from all the sobbing.

Mojo One came from somewhere right then and began licking my hand, and perhaps it was all the thinking about the angelic being planting that fern that startled me, but I sat up and cried out, "Ah!" like when someone is in a dark hallway and you didn't expect it.

My siblings turned, and if there was any consolation at all, it was that boys do not wear makeup because I'm sure I was quite a sight already, rushing past them, holding a book, tears flying. My sister engaged in this kind of behavior from time to time, but this was the first they'd seen it from me.

A boy learns much from watching a dog. A man can too. Overstating what the first Mojo taught me would be impossible. She helped shape my character, offering me a humble others-oriented model, a zest for the adventurous life. She schooled me in loyalty, something that would one day keep a limping marriage on the move until God could heal it. From the time I entered fifth grade until the year my first son was born, she modeled the ways of God. When I wandered, she waited faithfully for my return. When I needed encouragement, she showed up with some. She overlooked a barrelful of faults, never once threatening to leave, seeing past my outward appearance, reminding me each day that somebody somewhere loved me.

I am who I am thanks to the influence of parents and siblings and teachers and friends. And a ten-pound canine who taught me to open my eyes each day with expectancy. To look on life with purpose. And joy. Hoping for my Master's return.

Mojo II pointed me down a straight pathway through the toughest years of life, inciting me even at her ripe old age of fifteen to be courageous, to forgive quickly, to stop whining and holding grudges, to slow down, to be more patient. In many ways this wonderfully affable companion demonstrated a more Christlike attitude and love than most humans I know—including me.

Two dogs. Fifteen years each.

I don't recall a movie or book about a dog wherein the animal isn't laid to rest, but today I am happy to report that Mojo is alive and well beside me. Her muzzle has greyed, her body has thinned. She sleeps more than I'd like her to, and when she awakens I sense frustration at the time it takes her to rise and stretch. But even in this she is teaching me about adversity, preparing me for the days ahead. The end is never easy, but a life of loyalty, commitment, and faithfulness means the companionship of a family who cares and a legacy they'll celebrate for years to come.

Her eyes are clouded with age but unwavering when I look into them. A second glance and she is a puppy again. We are bringing her home and watching her attempt at escape. She is pouncing on me with unbridled enthusiasm. Bounding out front as I attempt to keep up—both of us eager for home. She is playing with my kids now, helping them grow up, helping them say goodbye. She can't speak, but she says, "You only get today. Today matters. Make it count."

Today the wind is whipping the tree branches, and rain is pelting the window. She needs her halting, leisurely stroll. I can still coax her to walk a mile by hiding tiny bits of apricot about the house, in the magazine rack, beneath a pillow, behind a plant. Her tail is wagging as the game begins.

Thank you, God, for the gift of a dog.

About the Author

Phil Callaway is the bestselling author of 25 books (including *Parenting: Don't Try This at Home*, *Making Life Rich Without Any Money*, and *To Be Perfectly Honest*). His humorous stories on family life have been featured in hundreds of magazines worldwide. His writings have been translated into Polish, Chinese, Spanish, German, Dutch, Indonesian, and English (one of which he speaks fluently).

Described as "Garrison Keillor crossed with my fourth-grade Sunday school teacher," Callaway is a popular speaker for corporations, educational conferences, churches, and marriage events. His radio show, *Laugh Again*, airs across North America, the UK, and English-speaking Africa. He is a frequent guest on national radio and television.

A self-described chocoholic, Phil's list of accomplishments includes muting the TV to listen to his children's questions (twice), taking out the garbage without being told (once), and convincing his high school sweetheart to marry him (once).

Visit Phil online at laughagain.org, or connect on Twitter (@philcallaway) and Facebook. For information on his speaking, email him at booking@laughagain.org.

Notes

Author's Note

1. The one million dog-bite victims are mostly children, and this counts only the ones who require medical attention. Dogs also kill 12 Americans a year. Insurance companies pay roughly $200 million each year in claims arising from dog bites.

Chapter 7: You Can Stay Where You Are

1. We then surveyed married couples, asking the same question. Actually we didn't, though such a study would be fascinating, wouldn't it? I would pay to read it.

2. Fanny Crosby also had four books of poetry published and two bestselling autobiographies. Though she was called the queen of gospel songwriters, she also cowrote popular secular songs as well as political and patriotic songs.

3. Annie Isabel Willis, "A Blind Hymn Writer," *Daily True American* (August 1, 1889), 2.

Chapter 10: Go Ahead and Howl

1. This was the highest registered response to any single question.

Chapter 11: Nothing Can Steal Your Joy

1. "In January 2011, a Border Collie was reported to have learned 1,022 words and acts consequently to human citation of those words." en.wikipedia.org/wiki/Border_Collie.

Chapter 12: The Best Is Still Out There

1. Genesis 2:19.

2. Genesis 7.

3. Jonah 4:11.

4. Revelation 19:14; Isaiah 65:25.

Chapter 13: Brighten Things for Others

1. In *A Better Brain at Any Age: The Holistic Way to Improve Your Memory, Reduce Stress, and Sharpen Your Wits* (Newburyport, MA: Conari Press, 2009), Sondra Kornblatt writes that humor is fast-acting. Less than a half-second after exposure to something funny, electrical waves move through the higher brain functions of the cerebral cortex. The limbic system makes you happier; the motor sections make you laugh. As well, the new field of gelotology (not to be confused with gelato, the Italian ice cream) claims that laughter helps the pituitary gland release its own pain-suppressing opiates and may even increase the response of cells that kill tumors and diseases. Unlike this author, Sondra does not mention being kicked out of seventh-grade health class.

Chapter 14: Only a Dog Loves You More than Himself

1. Psalm 56:13.

2. Psalm 18:19.

3. 2 Timothy 4:18.

Chapter 15: If Your Dog Is Fat, You May Be Too

1. Irene's father was one of the first to receive a successful kidney transplant. He passed away at the age of 48.

Chapter 17: Some Things Are Worth Chasing, Some Are Not

1. Mary MacVean, "For many people, gathering possessions is just the stuff of life," *Los Angeles Times*, March 21, 2014. articles.latimes.com/2014/mar/21/health/la-he-keeping-stuff-20140322.

2. Randy Frost and Gail Steketee are authors of *Stuff: Compulsive Hoarding and the Meaning of Things* (New York: Mariner Books, 2011). Frost says hoarders find "safety, comfort and value in their possessions."

Chapter 20: You Don't Have to Understand to Be Happy

1. Cesar Millan advises that such fear in our dogs can be remedied by thinking of yourself not so much as a dog owner but as a paramedic. He believes that when people feel bad, their dogs feel bad, which brings too many "negative energies" into the room. Cesar recommends calming oneself and then either putting the dog on a treadmill, saddling him with a backpack, or placing him in water in the bathtub. These may work, but I haven't tried them yet, believing that my wife and children will think I have lost my mind.

Chapter 21: We All Walk with a Limp

1. Not all of the dialogue in this book is verbatim, but this is. I can still remember where I was standing when he said this. The man is on his third marriage and later told me, "I should have stayed with my first wife. I just exchanged her for a new set of problems."

2. Ephesians 5:23-25.

Chapter 22: Humility Is like Underwear

1. Luke 18:9-14.

Chapter 25: Sometimes It's Nice to Be Patted

1. Proverbs 12:18.

Chapter 27: Bury the Right Things

1. Ephesians 4:31-32.

Chapter 28: Wag More, Bark Less

1. Carolyn Gregoire, "The 75-Year Study That Found the Secrets to a Fulfilling Life," *Huffington Post*, August 11, 2013. www.huffingtonpost.com/2013/08/11/how-this-harvard-psycholo_n_3727229.html.

2. According to the American Pet Products Manufacturer's Association, 63 percent of all US households have a pet. Topping the list are freshwater fish (142 million), then cats (88.3 million), and then dogs (74.8 million). Fish and cats are in more multi-pet homes than dogs—hence the careful wording of this statistic. Lynea Lattanzio, of Parlier, California, lives with more than seven hundred felines. She may be the reason someone I know boasts she has only seven cats (down from thirty).

Chapter 29: I Only Have Eyes for You

1. John M. Gottman and Nan Silver, *The Seven Principles for Making Marriage Work* (New York: Three Rivers Press, 1998), 5.

Chapter 30: Don't Jump from the Train

1. Ecclesiastes 7:10.

Chapter 31: Love Your Enemies

1. Please do not try this at home. This is a joke.
2. Susan Crauss Whitbourne, "Live Longer by Practicing Forgiveness," *Psychology Today*, January 1, 2013. www.psychologytoday.com/blog/fulfillment-any-age/201301/live-longer-practicing-forgiveness.
3. Ephesians 4:31.
4. Ephesians 4:32.

Chapter 32: The Best Treats Are Those You Don't Deserve

1. Russell and his wife now have two sons, aged 16 and 17. The younger has an interest in acting and modeling. He recently appeared with Wayne Gretzky in a Best Buy commercial and played a bit part in a documentary movie on Wayne's father, Walter. "We received the nicest letter from Walter Gretzky complimenting my son on his acting," "Russell told me. "I accidentally spilled coffee on it, but so far the helmet is fine."

Chapter 33: The Best Things Are Difficult

1. Psalm 56:1 NIV, 1984 edition.

Chapter 36: I Don't Have to Change You to Love You

1. Charles Colson, *The Faith* (Grand Rapids: Zondervan, 2008), 133-34.
2. I once wrote that our family went to a certain movie on opening night, a Thursday. I was rightly corrected. The movie opened on a Friday. Another disappointed reader called on Christmas morning. I had written about my friend's 1997 Ford Focus. "Ford didn't make them things until 1998." He too was right.
3. In *Who Was Jesus?* (Grand Rapids: Eerdmans, 1993), 63. N.T. Wright says, "Jewish revolutionaries whose leader had been executed by the authorities, and who managed to escape arrest themselves, had two options: give up the revolution, or find another leader. Claiming that the original leader was alive again was simply not an option. Unless, of course, he was."

Chapter 37: Never Overlook an Opportunity to Party

1. 2 Corinthians 4:16 NIV.
2. As much as possible I have tried to relay the details and chronology as accurately as possible. Technically the police did not tell me in person to slow down. I received a surprisingly sharp photo of my license plate in the mail, along with a request to send money.

Chapter 40: Don't Miss the Ocean for the Waves

1. Having endured a colonoscopy, I cannot help but wonder if nuclear laxatives are indeed available.
2. Tim Keller, "Christmas Message," available online at sermons2.redeemer.com/sermons/Christmas-message. "Throughout history," Keller says, "what has been considered wise has varied from age to age, but the truths of Christianity have stood and will stand forever."

Chapter 42: It's Okay to Ask

1. 2 Corinthians 1:8-9.